HOMEMADE HEALTHY DOG FOOD

The 2 in 1 Guide and Cookbook to Improve Your Furry Friend's Nutrition and Ensure Him a Long and Happy Life Discover Easy and Affordable Recipes for Meals and Treats

TRUDI RICHARDSON

Table of Contents

INTRODUCTION

When it comes to our beloved pets, their health and happiness are of utmost importance, and we're all passionate about ensuring our dogs thrive. A vital factor in achieving this is providing them with a well-balanced and nourishing diet. While numerous store-bought dog food options exist, an increasing number of pet owners now opt for crafting their own canine cuisine. And why wouldn't they? Homemade dog food offers a myriad of benefits that can truly revolutionize their furry companion's life.

In recent times, the trend of preparing wholesome dog food at home has soared, and rightly so. It equips dog owners with unparalleled authority over their pet's nourishment. Crafting a diet tailored to their unique requirements, preferences, and allergies becomes a breeze. By preparing dog food at home, you can meticulously select top-tier ingredients to guarantee your four-legged friend indulges in the most nutritious fare conceivable.

However, nutrition isn't the sole advantage. Homemade healthy dog food offers even more advantages. By incorporating fresh elements not commonly found in store-bought alternatives, such as prime meats, vibrant vegetables, and succulent fruits, you offer your pet an expanded array of nutrients, vitamins, and minerals. Crafting the food yourself grants you the ability to prepare smaller portions, affording better portion control and minimizing the risk of overindulgence.

Naturally, proper preparation and storage are crucial to safeguard your pet's well-being. Ensure meats are cooked thoroughly to eradicate any lurking bacteria. Stay vigilant about ingredients that can prove harmful to dogs, including onions, garlic, grapes, and chocolate. Store homemade dog food in airtight containers within the refrigerator or freezer to maintain its freshness and prevent spoilage.

Preparing homemade healthy dog food can be a great option for your furry friend's diet. Contrary to popular belief, it doesn't require daily cooking; you can cook a batch once every 1-3 weeks and store the arranged food properly. This approach saves time in the long run, making it more manageable than it may initially seem.

When you embark on the journey of crafting homemade healthy dog food, you aren't merely providing sustenance—you're nurturing your pet's overall welfare. Why settle for anything less than the absolute best? Seize control of your dog's diet and witness them thrive like never prior to.

WHY HOMEMADE DOG FOOD IS IMPORTANT

Homemade dog food is an absolute game-changer when it comes to boosting the health and happiness of our beloved canine buddies. While commercial dog food brands may seem convenient and offer an array of choices, homemade dog food brings a plethora of unmissable benefits that'll blow your mind.

First and foremost, homemade dog food puts you in the driver's seat, giving you complete control over the ingredients that go into your pup's grub. This level of control is absolutely crucial because it empowers you to handpick top-notch, nutrient-packed ingredients that cater to your furry friend's specific dietary requirements. You can customize their meals to cater to any allergies, sensitivities, or medical conditions, ensuring they get optimal nutrition without any sketchy additives or fillers. With this ultimate customization, your four-legged buddy will thrive, rocking peak health and enjoying a long, vibrant life.

Homemade dog food is your ticket to an adventure of flavors. Just like humans, dogs benefit immensely from a diverse range of nutrients derived from various food sources. By whipping up meals in your kitchen, you can switch up proteins, grains, fruits, and veggies, serving a well-rounded diet that mimics the natural feast of their ancestors. This epic variety not only tantalizes their taste buds but also delivers a wider spectrum of essential vitamins, minerals, and antioxidants vital for their immune system, organ function, and overall zest for life.

Say goodbye to artificial preservatives, additives, and subpar fillers that plague commercial dog food. These sneaky extras can wreak havoc on your pup's well-being, causing digestive woes, skin allergies, and even unwanted weight gain. But fear not! By preparing homemade meals, you can kick these harmful substances to the curb, minimizing the risk of health issues and ensuring your pooch's diet is devoid of unnecessary artificial junk.

Cooking up homemade dog food means taking control of food safety like a boss. Recent recalls of commercial pet food due to contamination or mishandling have sparked serious concerns about the safety of store-bought products. But fret not, superhero chef! By sourcing fresh ingredients and whipping up meals in your own kitchen, you can drastically diminish the chances of bacterial nasties creeping into your doggo's chow. This means their food will be safe, hygienic, and worry-free.

Whipping up homemade dog food fosters an unbreakable bond between you and your fluffy companion. Taking the time and effort to cook for your pup shows them just how much you love and cherish their well-being. It's an opportunity to nourish them with meals tailored to their individual preferences, showcasing your devotion in the most delicious way possible. Sharing homemade meals with your doggo fills your heart with a sense of satisfaction and fulfillment, taking the joy of pet ownership to a whole new level.

TYPES OF HOMEMADE HEALTHY DIET FOR DOGS

When it comes to homemade healthy diets for dogs, there are several popular approaches that pet owners may consider. These diets include the Biologically Appropriate Raw Food (BARF) diet, Prey Model Raw (PMR) diet, Do-It-Yourself (DIY) diets, and cooked homemade diets. Each approach has its own philosophy and guidelines, aiming to provide dogs with nutritionally balanced meals. Let's explore these diets in more detail:

BIOLOGICALLY APPROPRIATE RAW FOOD (BARF) DIET

The BARF diet is a popular approach to homemade dog food that aims to emulate the diet of dogs' wild ancestors. This diet is rooted in the belief that dogs are biologically designed to consume raw, natural foods. The BARF diet typically consists of a combination of raw meat, bones, organs, fruits, vegetables, and occasionally grains or dairy products.

The primary goal of the BARF diet is to provide dogs with a nutritionally balanced and diverse range of nutrients, similar to what they would have consumed in the wild. Raw meat, including muscle meat and organs, serves as the main protein source, supplying essential amino acids and promoting muscle development and maintenance. Bones are included to provide dental health benefits, as well as a natural source of calcium and other minerals.

Fruits and vegetables are incorporated into the BARF diet to provide necessary vitamins, minerals, and fiber. These plant-based components can contribute to overall health, immune system support, and digestion. Additionally, they include variety and palatability to the diet.

While the BARF diet primarily focuses on raw ingredients, some variations may include small amounts of grains or dairy products. Grains can serve as a source of carbohydrates, while dairy products may offer additional protein and fats. However, it's essential to note that not all BARF diet proponents include these components, as some believe that dogs have limited ability to digest grains and dairy.

PREY MODEL RAW (PMR) DIET

The PMR diet is a specific variation of the BARF diet that focuses on replicating the natural prey consumption of dogs. It emphasizes feeding dogs whole prey or parts of prey animals to provide a nutritionally balanced diet. Unlike the BARF diet, which includes a variety of ingredients, the PMR diet primarily consists of muscle meat, bones, and organs.

The core principle of the PMR diet is to mimic a dog's natural diet by offering them the entirety of a prey animal's body. This means including not only muscle meat but also bones and organs. The inclusion of bones in the diet serves as a source of calcium, phosphorus, and other minerals essential for a dog's skeletal health. Organs, such as liver, kidneys, and heart, provide vital nutrients like vitamins, minerals, and enzymes.

Unlike the BARF diet, the PMR diet does not typically include fruits, vegetables, grains, or dairy products. The focus is on providing dogs with the essential nutrients found in prey animals without additional plant-based or grain-based components. The belief is that dogs have evolved to thrive on a diet primarily consisting of animal-based ingredients.

DO-IT-YOURSELF (DIY) DIET

DIY diet for dogs involves the formulation and preparation of homemade dog food tailored to meet the specific needs of an individual dog. This approach allows pet owners to have full control over the ingredients, portion sizes, and customization of their dog's meals.

When opting for a DIY diet, it is crucial to carefully consider the nutritional requirements of dogs. A well-balanced diet should include adequate amounts of proteins, carbohydrates, fats, vitamins, and minerals. Proteins are essential for muscle development and repair, carbohydrates provide energy, fats contribute to overall health and coat condition, while vitamins and minerals support various bodily functions.

The flexibility of a DIY diet allows pet owners to choose high-quality ingredients based on their dog's preferences, dietary restrictions, and specific nutritional needs. This can include lean meats like chicken, turkey, or beef as protein sources, healthy carbohydrates such as sweet potatoes, brown rice, or quinoa, and beneficial fats from sources like fish or flaxseed oil. The inclusion of fruits and vegetables can provide additional vitamins, minerals, and fiber.

To ensure that a DIY diet is nutritionally balanced, it is essential to consult with a veterinarian or veterinary nutritionist. They can provide guidance on formulating a diet plan that meets the dog's specific requirements. This may involve calculating appropriate portion sizes, determining the right ratio of ingredients, and considering any underlying health conditions or dietary sensitivities.

COOKED HOMEMADE DIETS

Cooked homemade diets are a popular alternative to raw diets, where pet owners prepare and cook meals for their dogs using a variety of ingredients. Unlike raw diets, cooked homemade diets involve cooking the ingredients to enhance digestibility and eliminate potential bacterial risks.

When preparing cooked homemade diets, lean meats are commonly used as the primary source of protein. These can include options such as chicken, turkey, beef, or fish. The meats are cooked thoroughly to ensure they are safe for consumption. Cooking not only helps eliminate bacteria but also improves the digestibility of the proteins for dogs.

In addition to proteins, cooked homemade diets often include a combination of vegetables and grains. Vegetables like green beans, carrots, and sweet potatoes provide essential vitamins, minerals, and fiber. Grains such as brown rice, quinoa, or oats can serve as a source of carbohydrates, providing energy for dogs.

To ensure that cooked homemade diets are nutritionally balanced, it is essential to consider the specific dietary requirements of dogs. This may involve incorporating a variety of ingredients to provide the necessary vitamins, minerals, and essential fatty acids. Some pet owners may choose to include supplements, such as fish oil or multivitamins, to ensure their dogs receive all the essential nutrients.

Cooked homemade diets offer several benefits. They provide an alternative for pet owners who are uncomfortable feeding raw food to their dogs due to concerns about bacterial contamination. Cooking the ingredients can help eliminate potential pathogens, making the meals safer for both dogs and humans. Additionally, some dogs may find cooked meals more palatable and easier to digest.

BENEFITS OF MAKING YOUR OWN DOG FOOD

Making your own dog food offers several benefits that can contribute to the overall health and well-being of your furry friend. Here are some key advantages of preparing homemade dog food:

- Quality Control: Take charge of your dog's health by crafting your own dog food. Handpick premium, fresh ingredients that meet your dog's nutritional needs, avoiding subpar fillers, artificial additives, and unhealthy preservatives commonly found in commercial dog food.

- Customization: Tailor your furry friend's meals to perfection. Address dietary restrictions, allergies, or sensitivities with ease. You have the freedom to adjust portions and ingredients, ensuring a well-balanced blend of proteins, carbohydrates, and fats.
- Nutritional Balance: Unleash a spectrum of essential nutrients, vitamins, and minerals. Create a harmonious blend of proteins, grains, fruits, and vegetables that promotes optimal health, bolsters their immune system, and helps safeguard against health issues.
- Transparency: Shed light on the origins and composition of your dog's food. Hand-select and verify the quality of each ingredient, granting you peace of mind. Embrace the power of organic, locally sourced, or ethically raised ingredients.
- Digestive Health: Wave goodbye to digestive woes and food sensitivities. Identify and eliminate troublesome ingredients, promoting smoother digestion and reducing the risk of gastrointestinal problems. Say no to artificial additives and fillers for a healthier digestive system.
- Taste and Variety: Treat your dog's taste buds to a vibrant symphony of flavors, textures, and ingredients. Elevate mealtime with an enticing array of options, ensuring a well-rounded nutrient intake and preventing picky eating habits.
- Bonding and Engagement: Forge an unbreakable bond with your beloved pet. Engage them in the cooking process, turning meal preparation into a delightful shared experience. Demonstrate your love and care through the effort you invest in their nourishment.

While creating homemade dog food demands time, effort, and diligent research for optimal nutrition, the rewards of personalized, high-quality meals are immeasurable. Seek guidance from a veterinarian or professional veterinary nutritionist to curate balanced recipes tailored to your dog's unique requirements.

OVERVIEW OF THE BOOK

Homemade Healthy Dog Food is a comprehensive resource designed to educate and assist pet owners in preparing nutritious meals for their dogs. With its practical insights and collection of recipes, this book emphasizes the importance of homemade dog food and the benefits it can bring to our furry friends. By understanding the nutritional needs of dogs, pet owners can make informed choices about their diet and ensure they receive the best possible nutrition.

One of the book's main focuses is comparing homemade dog food to commercial options. It provides a thorough analysis of the advantages homemade food offers, such as better control over ingredients, customization based on individual needs, and the potential for improved overall health. By delving into the potential pitfalls of commercial dog food, the book encourages pet owners to consider the homemade alternative.

To assist readers in their journey, Homemade Healthy Dog Food offers a range of insights and guidance. It covers common mistakes that pet owners should avoid when preparing homemade dog food, ensuring the diet remains nutritionally balanced. The book highlights essential ingredients that should be included in a dog's diet, such as high-quality protein sources, healthy carbohydrates, and beneficial fats. It also provides tips on properly balancing these ingredients to meet a dog's specific nutritional requirements.

Moreover, the book emphasizes the significance of safe food handling practices. It educates readers on the importance of proper hygiene when preparing and storing homemade dog food, reducing the risk of bacterial contamination and ensuring the food remains fresh & safe for consumption. By following these guidelines, pet owners can provide their dogs with meals that are both nutritious and safe.

Homemade Healthy Dog Food also addresses the process of transitioning from a commercial diet to a homemade one. It offers step-by-step instructions on how to gradually introduce homemade food while minimizing digestive issues and allowing dogs to adapt to the new diet comfortably. Additionally, the book provides valuable insights for pet owners who need to manage specific dietary requirements or allergies, ensuring that homemade meals can accommodate various health conditions.

Throughout the book, frequently asked questions are answered, addressing common concerns and providing additional clarity on various aspects of homemade dog food. By addressing these queries, pet owners can feel more confident and well-informed as they embark on the journey of preparing homemade meals for their dogs.

Finally, this book presents a diverse range of recipes to suit different tastes & dietary needs. From breakfast options to satisfying dinners and even delicious treats, these recipes are designed to provide dogs with a variety of flavors and nutrients. For dogs with specific dietary requirements, specialized recipes are included, offering solutions for allergies, weight management, and other health concerns.

Kindly note that the recipes featured in this book serve as general guidelines, as each dog has unique nutritional requirements that need to be calculated specifically for them. This includes determining appropriate portion sizes tailored to each individual dog's needs.

UNDERSTANDING YOUR DOG'S NUTRITIONAL NEEDS

THE BASICS OF DOG NUTRITION

Maintaining the health and well-being of your beloved canine companion relies heavily on providing them with proper nutrition. Ensuring that homemade dog food satisfies their nutritional requirements is vital. A balanced diet for dogs should include the following elements.

Protein serves as the cornerstone of a dog's diet and should constitute a significant portion of their meals. Excellent sources of protein are lean meats like chicken, turkey, beef, or fish. These proteins contain essential amino acids that support muscle development and overall growth.

Carbohydrates are another essential component that provides energy for your dog. Opt for complex carbohydrates such as brown rice, sweet potatoes, or quinoa. These sources are more beneficial than simple carbohydrates found in processed foods.

Healthy fats play a vital role in a dog's diet by aiding nutrient absorption and promoting a healthy coat and skin. Include small amounts of olive oil, flaxseed oil, or fish oil to their meals to provide essential omega-3 fatty acids.

Fruits and vegetables offer valuable vitamins, minerals, and antioxidants. Choose dog-friendly options like carrots, green beans, spinach, or blueberries. Avoid using toxic foods such as grapes, raisins, onions, or garlic.

Calcium is essential for maintaining strong bones & teeth. You can provide this mineral by including dairy products like plain yogurt or cottage cheese. Alternatively, you can use powdered calcium supplements specifically formulated for dogs.

Supplementation may be necessary to fulfill specific nutritional requirements. Seek advice from your veterinarian to ascertain whether your dog requires any extra vitamins, minerals, or supplements for a well-rounded and healthy diet.

When preparing homemade dog food, it's crucial to avoid harmful ingredients like excessive salt, sugar, artificial additives, and spices. Additionally, certain foods are toxic to dogs, including chocolate, caffeine, alcohol, and some nuts.

Keep in mind that each dog has unique dietary needs based on factors such as age, size, breed, and overall health.

Regularly monitor your dog's weight, energy levels, coat condition, and overall health. Adjust the portion sizes and ingredients as needed to maintain a healthy weight and address any specific health concerns.

COMMON NUTRITIONAL DEFICIENCIES IN COMMERCIAL DOG FOOD

Commercial dog foods, despite claims of balanced nutrition, can still fall short in meeting essential dietary needs. Deficiencies in these products can manifest in various ways, including:

- Protein Insufficiency: Poor-quality dog foods may skimp on high-grade protein sources, leading to muscle weakness, stunted growth, and compromised immunity.
- Essential Fatty Acid Shortfall: Omega-3 and omega-6 fatty acids are vital for overall dog health, influencing skin, coat, joints, and brain function. Inadequate amounts of these critical fatty acids can be found in some commercial dog foods.
- Fiber Inadequacy: Proper digestion and a healthy gastrointestinal tract rely on sufficient fiber intake. Lack of fiber can result in distressing conditions like constipation, diarrhea, and various digestive issues.
- Vitamin and Mineral Deficits: Optimal levels of essential nutrients like vitamin A, vitamin D, vitamin E, and calcium may be lacking in commercial dog foods, leading to potential long-term health complications.
- Superfluous Fillers and Additives: Certain dog foods contain excessive amounts of low-nutrition fillers like corn, wheat, and soy. These additives contribute minimally to nutrition and may cause allergies, digestive problems, and weight gain.
- Artificial Additives: Many commercial dog foods incorporate artificial additives, including colors, flavors, and preservatives. These substances can have detrimental effects on dogs, triggering allergies or sensitivities.
- Contaminants: Certain dog food brands have been found to harbor harmful substances like heavy metals and toxins, posing risks to the well-being of dogs.

To mitigate the risk of nutritional deficiencies, it is crucial to opt for premium commercial dog foods that are specifically formulated to meet dogs' nutritional needs. Carefully reading ingredient lists and selecting products with identifiable meat sources, whole grains, and natural preservatives is advised. Additionally, diversifying your dog's nutrient intake by rotating between different brands and varieties can be beneficial. Regular consultation with a veterinarian is also recommended to ensure your dog's nutritional requirements are adequately addressed and any potential deficiencies are addressed promptly.

THE IMPORTANCE OF A BALANCED DIET

When it comes to homemade dog food, a balanced diet is absolutely vital for your furry companion's well-being. It's all about providing the perfect blend of nutrients, vitamins, and minerals to ensure optimal health. Here's why a balanced diet is so crucial with benefits:

Nutritional Adequacy: Your dog needs the right amount of proteins, carbs, fats, vitamins, and minerals to thrive. Each nutrient plays a unique role in preserving overall well-being, supporting bodily functions, and preventing pesky deficiencies or imbalances that can lead to health issues.

Energy and Vitality: Your dog's energy levels need a proper boost from nutrients. Carbs supply the energy, proteins foster muscle growth and repair, while fats offer concentrated fuel. A well-balanced diet, with the right ratios of these essential nutrients, powers up your dog, enhancing their liveliness and attentiveness.

Healthy Weight Management: Keeping your dog at an ideal weight is essential, and a balanced diet can help you achieve it. Obesity in dogs can lead to joint problems, diabetes, and heart disease. By providing balanced meals with appropriate portion sizes, you can help your dog maintain a healthy weight, dodging those weight-related complications.

Strong Immune System: Proper nutrition is the secret weapon for a resilient immune system. Vital nutrients like vitamins A, C, and E, along with zinc and selenium, strengthen immune function and shield your dog against infections, diseases, and other health challenges. A balanced diet loaded with immune-boosting nutrients empowers your dog to battle illnesses like a superhero.

Coat and Skin Health: A well-balanced diet works wonders for your dog's coat and skin. Omega-3 fatty acids, vitamin E, and biotin play starring roles in enhancing coat luster, preventing dryness, and curbing skin problems such as itchiness or flaking. Your pup will be the picture of canine radiance!

Digestive Health: A balanced diet with ample fiber content promotes proper digestion and gastrointestinal health. Fiber keeps bowel movements in check, preventing uncomfortable constipation or pesky diarrhea. It creates a harmonious gut environment, ensuring your dog's overall comfort and well-being.

Longevity and Disease Prevention: A lifelong balanced diet can be a key to a long and healthy life for your dog. It fortifies the body against diseases and decreases the risk of various health conditions. By nourishing your dog's body with care, they'll be better equipped to ward off illnesses and maintain top-notch health as they gracefully age.

Remember, the nutritional needs of dogs can vary based on factors like age, breed, size, and activity level. Consulting a veterinarian or a canine nutrition specialist ensures your homemade dog food is perfectly balanced and caters to their unique dietary requirements. Regularly monitor your dog's weight, body condition, and overall health, making any necessary diet adjustments along the way. Woof-worthy health is within reach!

HOMEMADE VS. COMMERCIAL DOG FOOD

COMPARISON OF HOMEMADE AND COMMERCIAL DOG FOOD

When it comes to nourishing your furry friend, you have two main choices: homemade dog food or commercial dog food. Let's compare the two options to help you make an informed decision:

Nutritional Control

- Homemade Dog Food: Take complete control by making dog food at home. You can tailor the diet to meet your dog's specific needs, selecting high-quality ingredients, adjusting protein, carbohydrates, and fats, and avoiding additives or fillers.
- Commercial Dog Food: Brands rigorously test and research their products to provide a balanced diet. However, ingredient quality and nutritional content may vary across brands and products.

Convenience

- Homemade Dog Food: Making homemade dog food requires time, effort, and meal planning. It involves purchasing ingredients, cooking and preparing meals, and ensuring proper storage and portioning. It's not as easy as pouring kibble into a container.
- Commercial Dog Food: Commercial dog food offers convenience with its availability in various forms (dry, wet, or freeze-dried). It can be easily purchased, stored, and served without extensive preparation. Perfect for busy pet owners or those with limited cooking capabilities.

Cost

- Homemade Dog Food: The cost of homemade dog food varies based on ingredient quality and availability. Opting for high-quality ingredients and supplements can make it more expensive than commercial options. However, if you select the correct ingredients, it is possible to obtain a high-quality product at a lower cost compared to commercially available feed. It requires some practice to develop an understanding of what and how to purchase for our diets.
- Commercial Dog Food: Commercial dog food comes in a range of prices, catering to different budgets. It offers predictability and affordability, especially with economy brands. However, premium or specialized formulas can be pricier.

Quality and Safety

- Homemade Dog Food: Preparing homemade dog food ensures you know exactly what goes into your dog's meals. You can choose fresh, high-quality ingredients and avoid potentially harmful additives. Proper hygiene and food safety practices are crucial to minimize bacterial contamination risks.

- Commercial Dog Food: Reputable brands follow strict quality control measures, testing their products to meet safety standards. Look for brands with a track record of using high-quality ingredients and maintaining safety protocols.

Special Dietary Needs

- Homemade Dog Food: Homemade dog food allows you to address specific dietary needs, such as allergies, sensitivities, or health conditions. You can tailor ingredients to accommodate these requirements and seek guidance from a veterinarian or canine nutritionist.
- Commercial Dog Food: Commercial dog food offers specialized formulas, like grain-free, limited ingredient, or hypoallergenic options. These formulas are designed to tackle common health issues, making it convenient for pet owners seeking targeted nutrition.

BENEFITS OF HOMEMADE DOG FOOD

Homemade dog food has several potential benefits for your canine companion. Here are some of the key advantages:

Ingredient Control: Take charge with homemade dog food and seize total control over the ingredients. Handpick fresh, high-quality components and customize the recipe to match your furry friend's dietary needs, preferences, and allergies. Wave goodbye to allergens, artificial additives, preservatives, and fillers commonly lurking in commercial dog food.

Nutritional Customization: Unleash the power of homemade dog food to craft a tailored and well-balanced diet. Achieve the perfect harmony of proteins, carbs, fats, vitamins, and minerals. Tackle specific health concerns like weight management, digestion, or allergies by meticulously selecting the ingredients and their proportions.

Freshness and Quality: Prepare homemade dog food and revel in the benefits of using the freshest, top-notch ingredients. Your pup will savor nutrient-rich meals bursting with wholesomeness. Fresh fare is especially kind to sensitive tummies or those dogs who struggle with common ingredients found in commercial dog food.

Variety and Palatability: Let homemade dog food introduce a symphony of ingredients and flavors to your pup's palate. Banish boredom and ignite a healthy appetite. By rotating proteins, veggies, and grains, you'll offer a doggie delicacy of diverse nutrients, textures, and tastes.

Bonding and Involvement: Whip up homemade dog food and forge an unbreakable bond with your four-legged friend. Get them involved in the process, let them sample ingredients, or lend a helping paw. Taking an active role in your dog's nutrition and well-being creates an extraordinary connection and fills your heart with joy and satisfaction.

Confidence in Quality: By crafting homemade dog food, you become the maestro of ingredients and cooking techniques. Rest easy, knowing your pup's meals are arranged with utmost care and quality. Tweak the recipe as needed based on their individual responses and nutritional requirements, and bask in the confidence that you're nourishing them just right.

RISKS OF COMMERCIAL DOG FOOD

Although commercial dog food is easily accessible and convenient, specific products may pose potential risks. It's essential to be aware of these risks and make informed choices when selecting commercial dog food. Here are some potential risks:

Quality and Sourcing: Not all commercial dog food brands maintain the same standards when it comes to ingredient quality and sourcing. Lower-quality brands may use inferior ingredients, such as by-products, fillers, or meat from questionable sources. These ingredients may lack the necessary nutritional value or even pose a higher risk of contamination.

Additives and Preservatives: Some commercial dog foods contain artificial additives, preservatives, colors, and flavors. These additives can potentially lead to allergic reactions, sensitivities, or digestive issues in certain dogs. Careful examination of ingredient labels and selecting brands that give priority to natural ingredients with minimal additives is crucial.

Nutritional Imbalances: While many commercial dog foods are formulated to meet the basic nutritional requirements of dogs, there can still be variations in the quality and balance of nutrients. Lower-quality brands may not provide sufficient levels of essential nutrients, leading to nutritional imbalances or deficiencies over time. It's essential to select reputable brands that undergo rigorous testing and meet nutritional standards.

Allergies & Sensitivities: Some dogs may develop allergies or sensitivities to specific ingredients commonly found in commercial dog food, such as grains, soy, or certain proteins. Identifying and managing these sensitivities can be challenging when relying solely on commercial options. In such cases, a homemade diet or specialized commercial formulas may be necessary.

Recalls and Contamination: Occasionally, commercial dog food brands may issue recalls due to potential contamination with harmful substances or pathogens. These recalls can be concerning for pet owners and highlight the importance of staying informed about product safety and monitoring official recall notices.

Lack of Individual Customization: Commercial dog food is formulated to cater to the general population of dogs, but each dog has unique dietary needs. It may not address specific health conditions, dietary preferences, or sensitivities that your dog may have. In such cases, a homemade diet or specialized formulas recommended by a veterinarian may be more suitable.

To mitigate these risks, it's essential to choose reputable commercial dog food brands that prioritize high-quality ingredients, have a track record of safety, and meet established nutritional standards. Regularly monitoring your dog's health, weight, and overall well-being is essential to ensure that the chosen commercial diet is appropriate and meets their individual needs.

COMMON MISTAKES TO AVOID

OVERFEEDING

Overfeeding your dog can wreak havoc on their health and well-being. It's crucial to grasp the dangers of excessive feeding and embrace portion control to keep your furry friend in top shape.

Overfeeding is a rampant issue among dog owners, often driven by a desire to express affection through food. However, its consequences can be detrimental. Weight gain is the most immediate effect, with extra calories being stored as fat, leading to canine obesity. This condition brings along various health concerns, including diabetes, cardiovascular ailments, joint complications, and a shorter lifespan.

Moreover, overfeeding can cause digestive problems as dogs can only process a certain amount of food at a time. Overwhelming their digestive system may result in indigestion, bloating, discomfort, and even vomiting or diarrhea.

Energy levels and vitality also suffer when dogs are overfed. Their bodies work harder to process excessive amounts of food, leading to lethargy, reduced activity levels, and a lack of energy. This sedentary lifestyle further contributes to weight gain.

Psychologically, overfed dogs may become overly dependent on food for comfort and exhibit behavioral issues like begging, food guarding, or an obsession with food. Their appetite for regular meals may decrease, leading to imbalances in nutrient intake and potential nutritional deficiencies.

To prevent overfeeding, practice portion control and establish a regular feeding routine. Consult with a veterinarian to determine the appropriate portion sizes and feeding frequency based on factors like age, breed, size, activity level, and health. Commercial dog food packaging provides feeding guidelines based on weight, but monitoring your dog's body condition is essential for adjusting portion sizes.

Accurate measurement of food using a scale or measuring cup is crucial. Avoid free-feeding and establish regular mealtimes with appropriate portions. Instead of relying on food for affection or reward, incorporate other forms of positive reinforcement like praise, playtime, or affectionate attention.

Keep in mind that some dogs may have specific dietary requirements due to health conditions or special needs. Working closely with a veterinarian or canine nutritionist is essential to develop a feeding plan that meets those requirements without overfeeding.

UNDERFEEDING

Underfeeding your dog can seriously harm their health and overall well-being. It's vital to provide your furry companion with adequate nourishment to meet their dietary needs and maintain a balanced physique. Underfeeding occurs when dogs receive insufficient food, either in terms of portion size or frequency, resulting in various health issues.

Consistently underfeeding a dog denies them the necessary calories to support their daily energy requirements. This can lead to weight loss and malnutrition. Dogs rely on a balanced intake of proteins, carbohydrates, fats, vitamins, and minerals to thrive. Without enough of these essential nutrients, their body functions suboptimally, causing a range of health problems.

Weight loss is an immediate consequence of underfeeding. Dogs may become visibly thinner, with prominent ribcages and spines. While weight loss can be beneficial for overweight dogs, excessive or rapid weight loss due to underfeeding indicates malnourishment and muscle wasting. Lethargy, weakness, and reduced stamina are also common signs as their body struggles with low energy levels.

Insufficient nourishment puts dogs at a higher risk of having a weakened immune system, making them more susceptible to infections, diseases, and slower healing. A well-balanced intake of vital vitamins and minerals is crucial for the proper functioning of the immune system. Without adequate nutrition, dogs may experience frequent illnesses, prolonged recovery periods, and a compromised ability to fight off pathogens.

Malnutrition resulting from underfeeding can lead to deficiencies in specific nutrients. For example, inadequate protein intake can cause muscle wasting, weakness, and poor growth. Protein plays a critical role in the development and maintenance of muscles, tissues, and organs. Without enough protein, dogs may experience reduced muscle mass, delayed wound healing, and an overall weakened physique.

Underfeeding negatively affects a dog's coat and skin health. Essential fatty acids like omega-3 and omega-6 are vital for maintaining a nourished coat, flexible skin, and preventing dryness or irritation. Insufficient intake of these fatty acids can result in a dull, dry coat, flaky skin, and increased vulnerability to skin infections or allergies.

Digestive issues are also common among underfed dogs. Inadequate dietary fiber intake may lead to constipation or irregular bowel movements, causing discomfort and the risk of digestive obstructions. Fiber plays a crucial role in maintaining a healthy digestive system and regular bowel movements. Without enough fiber, dogs may suffer from gastrointestinal problems like diarrhea or constipation.

Underfeeding can have long-term effects on a dog's growth and development, especially in puppies. Insufficient nutrition during critical growth stages can lead to stunted growth, weak bones, and skeletal abnormalities. Proper nutrition is essential to support the rapid development of puppies' bodies and ensure healthy bone formation. Inadequate nutrition can impair their growth and result in long-term health complications.

It's essential to remember that each dog has unique nutritional requirements based on factors such as age, breed, size, and activity level. Feeding guidelines provided by the manufacturer should serve as a starting point, but adjustments may be necessary to meet your dog's specific needs. Consulting with a veterinarian can help determine the appropriate portion sizes and feeding frequency for your dog.

INCOMPLETE NUTRITION

Incomplete nutrition in dogs refers to a situation where their diet fails to provide all the necessary nutrients in adequate amounts to support optimal health and well-being. This can occur with both homemade and commercial dog food if they lack proper formulation or quality control. Incomplete nutrition can have detrimental effects on a dog's overall health, growth, immune system, and can lead to various health issues.

A well-balanced diet is essential for dogs to thrive and meet their nutritional requirements. It should include the right proportions of proteins, carbohydrates, fats, vitamins, minerals, and water. When any of these essential components are deficient or imbalanced, it can result in incomplete nutrition and subsequent health problems.

Proteins are crucial for dogs as they provide amino acids necessary for tissue repair, growth, and maintenance. Incomplete protein intake can lead to muscle weakness, poor growth, and compromised immune function. Dogs require high-quality protein sources like meat, fish, or eggs to meet their protein needs. If the diet lacks these essential proteins, it can result in incomplete nutrition and associated health issues.

Dogs rely on carbohydrates as an energy source, and they also obtain fiber from them, which helps with digestion and maintains regular bowel movements. Insufficient consumption of carbohydrates can result in insufficient energy levels and gastrointestinal issues like constipation or diarrhea. Dogs can obtain carbohydrates from sources like whole grains, fruits, and vegetables. A lack of these essential carbohydrates in the diet can result in incomplete nutrition and associated health complications.

Fats play a crucial role in a dog's diet as they offer energy, support cell function, and help absorb fat-soluble vitamins. Incomplete fat intake can lead to a lack of energy, dry skin, a dull coat, and deficiencies in fat-soluble vitamins. Dogs need a proper mix of omega-3 and omega-6 fatty acids, which can be acquired from options such as fish oil or flaxseed oil. If these essential fats are not provided in sufficient amounts, it can result in incomplete nutrition and subsequent health issues.

Vitamins and minerals are vital for dogs' overall health and well-being. Incomplete intake of these essential nutrients can lead to various shortages and associated health problems. For example, vitamin A deficiency can cause vision problems, skin issues, and a weakened immune system. Incomplete intake of calcium and vitamin D can result in bone disorders and poor skeletal development. Vitamins & minerals can be gained from a well-formulated diet that comprises a diversity of fruits, vegetables, and fortified ingredients. Inadequate amounts of these vital nutrients in a dog's diet can result in incomplete nutrition and related health complications.

Water is a crucial nutrient for dogs, and inadequate hydration can also contribute to incomplete nutrition. Water is necessary for proper digestion, circulation, temperature regulation, and overall body function. Insufficient hydration can result in a range of health complications such as impaired organ function, urinary problems, and heatstroke. It is crucial to have constant access to clean, fresh water to maintain proper hydration and avoid inadequate nutrition caused by a lack of water.

Both homemade and commercial dog foods can be at risk of incomplete nutrition if not properly formulated or quality-controlled. Homemade diets, while offering flexibility and customization, require careful planning and knowledge of canine nutritional needs. Without proper formulation or guidance from a veterinarian or canine nutritionist, homemade diets can lack essential nutrients and result in incomplete nutrition.

Commercial dog foods also vary in quality, with some brands prioritizing proper formulation and others using lower-quality ingredients and fillers. It's essential to choose reputable brands that undergo rigorous testing, have good quality control measures, and meet established nutritional standards. Reading the ingredient list and selecting products with named meat sources, whole grains, and natural preservatives is advisable.

To avoid incomplete nutrition, it's essential to ensure that your dog's diet is properly balanced and provides all the necessary nutrients. Regular consultation with a veterinarian or canine nutritionist can help ensure that your dog's diet meets their specific needs and supports optimal health. Regular monitoring of your dog's weight, body condition, and overall well-being is crucial to identify any signs of incomplete nutrition or deficiencies and make necessary adjustments to their diet.

COMMON FOODS THAT ARE TOXIC TO DOGS

Dog owners should possess knowledge about commonly toxic foods for dogs. While this is not an exhaustive list, below are the foods that are generally considered toxic to dogs:

- **Chocolate:** Contains theobromine and caffeine, which are toxic to dogs. Dark chocolate and unsweetened baking chocolate are more dangerous than milk chocolate due to higher levels of these compounds.
- **Grapes & raisins:** Can cause kidney failure in dogs. Even small amounts can be life-threatening.
- **Onions and garlic:** All forms can damage a dog's red blood cells and cause anemia. Toxicity can occur gradually or with a large ingestion.
- **Xylitol:** Found in sugar-free products like gum, candy, and baked goods. Can rapidly induce insulin discharge, leading to low blood sugar, liver issues, and potentially fatal consequences.
- **Alcohol:** Causes intoxication, vomiting, loss of coordination, tremors, and in severe cases, respiratory failure.
- **Caffeine:** Similar to chocolate, caffeine is toxic to dogs. It can cause restlessness, rapid breathing, heart palpitations, muscle tremors, and seizures.
- **Avocado:** Contains persin, which causes vomiting, diarrhea, and pancreatitis. Avocado pits are choking hazards.
- **Macadamia nuts:** Causes weakness, tremors, and potentially life-threatening reactions. Even small amounts can lead to vomiting, fever, and elevated heart rate.
- **Raw meat, bones, and fat trimmings:** Can cause food poisoning, intestinal blockages, injuries, and pancreatitis.
- **Dairy products:** Many dogs are lactose intolerant and may experience digestive upset from dairy products.
- **Cinnamon:** Large amounts or cinnamon essential oil can irritate a dog's mouth, digestive system, lower blood sugar levels, and lead to liver disease.

- **Salt:** Excessive salt intake leads to electrolyte imbalances and dehydration in dogs. Avoid feeding salty snacks or processed foods.
- **Nutmeg:** Contains myristicin, which causes hallucinations, tremors, seizures, and a high heart rate.
- **Mushrooms:** Certain varieties of mushrooms are toxic to dogs. Prevent them from ingesting any wild mushrooms.
- **Chives and Leeks:** All members of the Allium family, including chives, leeks, and shallots, are toxic to dogs. They contain compounds that can damage a dog's red blood cells and lead to anemia. Ingestion of chives or leeks can cause symptoms such as vomiting, diarrhea, abdominal pain, and weakness.
- **Rhubarb:** Rhubarb leaves contain oxalates, which are toxic to dogs. Ingesting rhubarb leaves can cause kidney damage, gastrointestinal upset, and even neurological symptoms. Keep dogs away from rhubarb plants and ensure they cannot access any discarded leaves.
- **Persimmons, Peaches, and Plums:** The seeds, pits, and leaves of persimmons, peaches, and plums contain compounds that can be toxic to dogs. Ingestion of these parts can cause gastrointestinal obstruction and intestinal issues. It's best to remove seeds, pits, and leaves prior to offering these fruits to your dog.
- **Raw Eggs:** Raw eggs pose a risk of salmonella and E. coli contamination. They can also interfere with biotin absorption, leading to a biotin deficiency in dogs. It's generally recommended to avoid feeding raw eggs to dogs and opt for cooked eggs instead.
- **Yeast:** Consuming yeast dough can cause a dog's stomach to expand, leading to bloating and discomfort. The yeast fermentation process also produces alcohol, which can result in alcohol poisoning. Keep yeast products away from your dog.
- **Tea:** While tea can be a soothing beverage for humans, it can be toxic to dogs due to its caffeine content. It's essential to prevent your canine companion from accessing your tea cup and also keep them away from tea bags that might end up in the trash or compost pile.
- **Moldy or Spoiled Foods:** Moldy or spoiled foods can contain toxins that are harmful to dogs. Consumption of these foods can lead to gastrointestinal upset, neurological issues, or even organ failure. Make sure to discard any food that shows signs of mold or spoilage.
- **Soda:** Keep your pup away from the soda as well, since it can be a source of caffeine. Some sodas, especially if they are labeled as sugar-free, also contain xylitol. Both caffeine and xylitol are toxic to dogs.

Remember that dogs have varying sensitivities. If your dog consumes toxic food or shows signs of poisoning, contact a veterinarian immediately. Take preventive measures, keep hazardous foods out of reach, educate yourself about risks, and consult your veterinarian for guidance.

ESSENTIAL INGREDIENTS FOR HOMEMADE DOG FOOD

PROTEINS

Proteins are an essential component of a homemade dog food diet and play a vital role in supporting your dog's overall health and well-being. Amino acids, the essential components of proteins, play a vital role in numerous bodily functions. These functions encompass tissue growth and repair, enzyme and hormone production, as well as immune system functionality. Incorporating high-quality proteins into your dog's homemade diet ensures they receive the necessary amino acids to thrive.

When selecting proteins for your homemade dog food, it's essential to consider both the source and the quality of the protein. Dogs typically prefer animal-based proteins since they provide a balanced combination of essential amino acids. Some common animal-based protein sources suitable for homemade dog food include:

- Lean Meats: Chicken, turkey, beef, lamb, and pork are protein-packed pals for your dog. Just cook 'em up good to keep those pesky pathogens away and make digestion a breeze. Trim off extra fat and skin because too much fat can upset some tummies and cause pancreatitis.

- Fish: Salmon, trout, sardines, and mackerel are like oceanic superheroes. They're loaded with high-quality protein and omega-3 fatty acids. Omega-3s are like the chill pill for your dog's coat, skin, and joints. Watch out for fish bones, though—they're party poopers and can cause choking or ouchies. Eliminate 'em prior to serving.

- Eggs: Eggs are the complete protein package, with all the amino acids your dog needs to rock and roll. Plus, they're packed with vitamins and minerals. Cook those eggs up and mix 'em into your pup's food for a protein boost. But remember, fully cooked eggs are the way to go to dodge any salmonella risks.

- Dairy Products: Some dogs can handle a bit of dairy fun, like plain yogurt or cottage cheese. These tasty treats bring protein and probiotics to the party, keeping your dog's tummy in tip-top shape. But not all dogs can handle dairy, so keep an eye on your pal's reaction and chat with your vet for advice.

- Organ Meats: Liver, kidneys, and heart are nutritional powerhouses that deliver essential vitamins and minerals. They're like the MVPs of homemade meals. Just don't go overboard with 'em, as too much can mess with specific nutrients. Cook 'em up and include 'em to your pup's plate for a nutrition boost.

  Organ meats can be cooked and incorporated into your dog's homemade meals to enhance the nutritional value.

When including protein in your dog's homemade diet, it's essential to ensure that the overall balance of the diet is appropriate. The protein content should be balanced with carbohydrates and fats to meet your dog's specific needs. Seek advice from a veterinarian or a specialist in canine nutrition to ascertain the ideal ratio of protein, carbohydrates, and fats for your dog, taking into consideration factors such as their age, size, activity level, and any existing health conditions.

In addition to selecting high-quality protein sources, it's also crucial to provide variety in your dog's protein options. Offering a range of proteins ensures that your dog receives a diverse array of essential amino acids and other nutrients. Rotating proteins can also help prevent the development of allergies or sensitivities to specific protein sources.

It is crucial to adhere to appropriate food safety measures when preparing proteins for your dog's homemade diet. Thoroughly cook all meats to eliminate potential bacteria or parasites that may be harmful to your dog. Avoid using seasonings, spices, or additives that may be toxic to dogs. Additionally, be mindful of bones, especially small and brittle bones that can splinter and cause choking hazards or intestinal blockages. If you choose to include bones, they should be raw, large, and suitable for consumption under supervision.

CARBOHYDRATES

Carbohydrates, a must-have for a well-rounded diet in dogs, are also vital in homemade dog food recipes. Despite being mainly carnivores, dogs can still benefit from a moderate amount of carbohydrates. These nutrients provide energy, fiber, and essential elements that support overall health. By carefully selecting and incorporating carbohydrates into homemade dog food, you can create a balanced and nutritious meal for your furry friend.

Carbohydrates play a crucial role in providing dogs with energy. Glucose, derived from carbohydrate breakdown, acts as the primary energy source for cells in their bodies. Dogs require energy for daily activities, exercise, and bodily functions. Although dogs tolerate low-carbohydrate diets better than humans, carbohydrates still play a significant role in meeting their energy needs.

Moreover, carbohydrates supply dietary fiber, which is essential for promoting healthy digestion. Fiber adds bulk to their diet, aiding regular bowel movements and preventing constipation. It also fosters the growth of beneficial microorganisms in their gastrointestinal tract, ensuring a well-functioning digestive system. Sufficient fiber intake helps regulate stool consistency and improves overall digestive health.

Including carbohydrates in homemade dog food helps achieve a balanced macronutrient profile. A well-crafted recipe typically combines protein, carbohydrates, and fats. Carbohydrates help balance the diet's calorie content, ensuring dogs receive enough energy while maintaining an appropriate weight. They also prevent excessive protein intake, which can strain the kidneys over time.

Carbohydrates are a valuable source of essential vitamins and minerals. While dogs have different nutritional requirements compared to humans, they still need certain nutrients found in plant-based sources. Carbohydrate-rich ingredients like vegetables and fruits provide vital vitamins, including vitamin A, vitamin C, and various B vitamins. These vitamins support the immune system, promote good vision, maintain healthy skin, and contribute to overall well-being.

Furthermore, carbohydrates contribute to the overall palatability and variety of homemade dog food. Including a range of carbohydrate sources adds diverse textures, flavors, and nutritional benefits to their diet. Dogs, like humans, appreciate and benefit from a diverse range of ingredients in their meals. Mixing different carbohydrate sources such as whole grains, legumes, and vegetables creates a well-rounded and interesting diet for your dog.

When selecting carbohydrates for homemade dog food, it is essential to choose appropriate sources that offer nutritional value and are safe for dogs. Whole grains like brown rice, quinoa, oats, and barley are commonly used as carbohydrate sources. These grains provide complex carbohydrates, dietary fiber, and various vitamins and minerals. It is crucial to cook grains thoroughly to ensure proper digestion and nutrient availability.

In addition to grains, vegetables and fruits can also serve as valuable carbohydrate sources. Fiber-rich vegetables such as sweet potatoes, carrots, green beans, peas, and pumpkin offer vitamins and antioxidants. Moderation is key when including fruits like apples, blueberries, and bananas to provide additional nutrients and natural sweetness.

When incorporating carbohydrates into homemade dog food, it is crucial to consider portion sizes and individual dog's needs. Each dog has unique dietary requirements based on factors such as age, size, breed, activity level, and existing health conditions.

It is essential to understand that not all carbohydrates are suitable for dogs, and certain ingredients should be avoided. Dogs have limited capacity to digest specific carbohydrates, especially those with a high glycemic index like white bread, white rice, or heavily processed grains. These ingredients can cause rapid surges in blood sugar levels, potentially leading to weight gain or other health problems.

Additionally, it is crucial to avoid using ingredients that are toxic to dogs, even if they contain carbohydrates. Onions, garlic, and grapes, for example, should not be included in homemade dog food as they can be toxic. Thorough research is necessary to ensure the ingredients you choose are safe and suitable for dogs.

FATS

Fats are an essential ingredient in homemade dog food due to their numerous vital roles in a dog's overall health and well-being. While often given a negative connotation in human nutrition, fats play a crucial role in providing energy, supporting organ function, promoting healthy skin and coat, aiding nutrient absorption, and contributing to overall cell and immune system health in dogs. When formulating homemade dog food, it is essential to include the right types and amounts of fats to ensure a balanced and nutritious diet for your furry friend.

One of the primary functions of fats in a dog's diet is to provide energy. Fats are a concentrated source of calories and provide more than twice the energy of proteins and carbohydrates. Dogs require a certain amount of dietary fat to fuel their daily activities, maintain proper body weight, and support metabolic processes. Without adequate fat intake, dogs may experience lethargy, weight loss, and an overall lack of energy. Including the right amount of healthy fats in homemade dog food helps ensure that dogs receive the necessary energy to lead an active and healthy lifestyle.

Healthy fats are essential for dogs to have healthy skin and a glossy coat. They contribute to the preservation of the skin barrier, prevent dryness, and decrease inflammation. The presence of fatty acids, particularly omega-3 and omega-6, is crucial for maintaining optimal skin well-being. Omega-3 fatty acids, which can be obtained from fish oil and flaxseed oil, possess anti-inflammatory qualities that can provide relief from skin allergies and irritations. Omega-6 fatty acids, present in oils like sunflower oil or safflower oil, help maintain the skin's natural moisture and promote a healthy coat. Including these essential fatty acids in homemade dog food can significantly contribute to the overall skin and coat health of your furry companion.

In addition to energy and skin health, fats play a critical role in supporting various organ functions in dogs. They provide protection and insulation for organs, aiding in shock absorption and maintaining proper temperature regulation. Fats also serve as a carrier for fat-soluble vitamins (A, D, E, and K) and facilitate their absorption. These vitamins are crucial for various bodily functions, including vision, bone health, antioxidant protection, and blood clotting. Including adequate amounts of healthy fats in homemade dog food ensures that these essential vitamins are properly absorbed and utilized by the body.

Furthermore, fats are essential for the proper functioning of the nervous system in dogs. The myelin sheath, which surrounds and protects nerve cells, is composed of fats. Adequate fat intake is necessary to support proper nerve transmission, coordination, and overall neurological health. Without sufficient fat in the diet, dogs may experience neurological issues, including weakness, tremors, and poor coordination. Including the right types of fats, such as those found in fish oil or other sources rich in omega-3 fatty acids, can contribute to optimal brain and nerve function in dogs.

Fats also play a vital role in the immune system of dogs. They support the production of immune cells and help regulate inflammation. Certain types of fats, like the medium-chain triglycerides (MCTs), have antimicrobial and antiviral properties that can enhance immune function. MCTs are found in coconut oil and can be a valuable addition to homemade dog food recipes, especially for dogs with compromised immune systems or those recovering from illnesses.

When incorporating fats into homemade dog food, it is essential to choose the right types of fats and maintain a proper balance. Healthy fats include sources like lean meats, fish, poultry, eggs, flaxseed oil, fish oil, and coconut oil. It is recommended to choose lean cuts of meat and remove extra fat prior to including them in homemade dog food recipes to prevent excessive calorie intake. Moderation is key, as an excessive amount of fat can lead to weight gain and related health issues. Consultation with a veterinarian or canine nutritionist can provide valuable guidance in determining the appropriate amount and types of fats to include in your dog's homemade diet based on their individual needs, age, activity level, and overall health condition.

VITAMINS AND MINERALS

Vitamins and minerals are absolute game-changers for your dog's health and well-being. They are like the secret weapons that power various functions in their body, from metabolism and immune system strength to bone health and cellular processes. So, when you're whipping up some homemade dog food, it's absolutely crucial to make sure you're serving up the perfect balance of these vital nutrients to cater to your furry friend's unique needs.

Let's start with vitamins, those essential organic superheroes that are needed in small quantities to work their magic. They team up with enzymes in the body, acting as coenzymes to make sure all the essential chemical reactions run smoothly. There are two vitamin categories: fat-soluble vitamins (vitamin A, D, E, and K) and water-soluble vitamins (vitamin C and B-complex vitamins).

Fat-soluble vitamins are the cool kids who hang out in fatty tissues and the liver. They are the powerhouses behind a strong immune system, sharp vision, sturdy bones, and antioxidant protection. Vitamin A is like the superstar promoting vision, growth, and immune function. Vitamin D takes charge of calcium absorption and is all about bone health. Vitamin E swoops in as an antioxidant to shield cells from harm. And then we have vitamin K, the MVP for blood clotting and bone metabolism. To make sure your dog gets a healthy dose of these fat-soluble vitamins, include sources like liver, fish oil, egg yolks, and leafy green veggies in their homemade meals.

Water-soluble vitamins are a different breed. They aren't stored in the body, so it's all about regular dietary intake. These vitamins are crucial for energy metabolism, immune system support, and overall well-being. Vitamin C is the mighty antioxidant, backing up the immune system and helping with collagen synthesis. The B-complex vitamins, including the likes of thiamine (B1), riboflavin (B2), niacin (B3), pantothenic acid (B5), pyridoxine (B6), biotin (B7), folic acid (B9), and cobalamin (B12), are all about energy production, nervous system function, and making red blood cells. Fruits, vegetables, and organ meats are your go-to sources for these water-soluble vitamins.

Now, let's talk minerals. These inorganic elements are like the unsung heroes, silently pulling strings behind the scenes. They're involved in bone formation, enzyme activation, muscle contractions, nerve function, and fluid balance. Minerals fall into two groups: macrominerals and trace minerals.

Macrominerals are the big players that the body needs in larger quantities. Calcium and phosphorus are the dynamic duo for bone and teeth development, nerve function, and muscle contractions. Potassium, sodium, and chloride are the powerhouses maintaining fluid balance, supporting nerves, and making sure those muscles contract like they should. Magnesium is the key player in enzyme function and energy production. To give your pup a generous helping of macrominerals, include meat, fish, dairy products, and certain fruits and veggies in their homemade meals.

Trace minerals may be small, but they're no less essential for overall health. Iron is all about oxygen transport and red blood cell production. Zinc takes charge of immune function, wound healing, and keeping the skin in tip-top shape. Copper plays its part in forming connective tissue and handling iron metabolism. Manganese is like the bone builder and antioxidant defender. Selenium steps in as an antioxidant and keeps the thyroid ticking. Speaking of the thyroid, iodine is the essential ingredient for thyroid hormone synthesis, while chromium plays a role in glucose metabolism. To make sure your pup gets enough trace minerals, include organ meats, seafood, eggs, and certain veggies in their homemade meals.

When you're whipping up homemade dog food, make sure to mix things up and offer a variety of ingredients packed with a wide range of vitamins and minerals. One food alone won't cut it. Your pup needs a diverse menu of top-notch animal proteins, whole grains, fruits, veggies, and healthy fats to get a well-rounded supply of these essential nutrients. But remember, the specific requirements may vary based on your dog's age, breed, size, activity level, and any underlying health conditions.

Lastly, don't forget about the proper preparation and storage of homemade dog food. You want to preserve those precious vitamins and minerals. Avoid overcooking or exposing the food to too much warm, as it can lead to nutrient loss. Opt for light cooking or steaming to retain the nutritional value of veggies. And to ensure a full spectrum of vitamins and minerals, mix it up with fresh ingredients and rotate the protein sources in your dog's diet.

SUPPLEMENTS

Certain supplements are essential to complement a natural dog food diet. Additional supplements may be necessary if you cannot offer a diverse range of foods or if certain food groups are excluded. Furthermore, the longer the food is cooked or frozen, the more nutrients are depleted. Here are some recommended dog supplements:

1. Calcium: Calcium ought to be included to your dog's homemade food regardless of whether or not it contains (RMBs), which are an excellent source of calcium. The amounts of calcium that are often found in multivitamins and mineral supplements are insufficient. Calcium content should be between 800 and 1,000 milligrams per pound of food, excluding non-starchy vegetables. You can use any simple source of calcium, like powdered eggshells (about half a tsp of powdered eggshells has 1,000 milligrams of calcium). Animal Essences' Seaweed Calcium is also a beneficial option for additional minerals. Note that the list of calcium-rich foods provided is intended for humans and includes orange juice, which should be avoided for dogs due to its acidity and potential stomach upset.

2. Oils: Most homemade diets need the addition of oils to provide necessary fats, calories, and specific nutrients. It is crucial to select the appropriate oils as each type supplies various nutrients.

a) Fish Oil: Fish oil for dogs contains EPA and DHA, omega-3 fatty acids that aid in immune system regulation and inflammation reduction. Provide an amount that supplies approximately 300 mg of combined EPA and DHA per twenty-thirty lbs. of body weight on days when fish is not included in the diet. Exercise caution with liquid fish oil supplements as they may recommend higher doses, leading to excessive fat calories.

b) Cod Liver Oil: Cod liver oil offers vitamins A and D, as well as EPA and DHA. If your dog's diet lacks sufficient fish, provide cod liver oil in an amount that delivers around 400 IU of vitamin D daily for a 100-pound dog (proportionally less for smaller dogs). It can be combined with other fish oil supplements to increase the levels of EPA and DHA if desired.

c) Plant Oils: Linoleic acid is an important omega-6 fatty acid, and if your dog's diet doesn't comprise considerable levels of poultry fat, which can be discovered in dark meat and skin, then your dog might be deficient in this nutrient. If this is the case, you can supplement your diet with linoleic acid by using oil derived from walnuts, hempseed, corn, vegetables (soybeans), or safflower that is high in linoleic acid. Add approximately one teaspoon of oil per pound of meat and other animal products; if utilizing canola or sunflower oil, twice the dose that is called for in the previous sentence. Although olive oil and high-oleic safflower oil are low in omega-6 and hence cannot serve as a substitute, if extra fat is needed, modest quantities of each might be included to the recipe. Coconut oil, predominantly containing saturated fats, could be utilized in conjunction with other oils, but not as a substitute.

HOW TO PROPERLY BALANCE YOUR DOG'S DIET

UNDERSTANDING MACRONUTRIENTS AND MICRONUTRIENTS

Properly balancing your dog's diet involves understanding the importance of macronutrients and micronutrients. Macronutrients are the major components of a dog's diet and include proteins, carbohydrates, and fats. Proteins play a crucial role in the development and restoration of cells, supplying the essential amino acids needed to support muscle growth, as well as overall well-being. High-quality animal-based proteins, such as those from meat, fish, and eggs, are particularly beneficial for dogs.

Dogs rely on carbohydrates as a crucial source of energy, supplying them with the necessary fuel to carry out their daily tasks. While dogs are primarily carnivorous, they can still benefit from moderate amounts of carbohydrates obtained from sources like whole grains, fruits, and vegetables. However, it's essential to choose complex carbohydrates over simple sugars to avoid blood sugar spikes.

Fats are crucial for various bodily functions and serve as a concentrated energy source. They assist in the assimilation of vitamins that dissolve in fat, promote the well-being of the skin and fur, and play a role in the production of hormones. High-quality fats derived from animal-based sources, such as fish oil and chicken fat, are beneficial for dogs.

Micronutrients are essential vitamins and minerals that dogs require in smaller amounts but are equally essential for their overall health. These include vitamins A, D, E, and K, as well as various B vitamins. Minerals like calcium, phosphorus, magnesium, and potassium are vital for bone health, muscle function, and electrolyte balance. A diverse range of fruits, vegetables, and whole foods in one's diet allows for the acquisition of micronutrients.

Consulting with a veterinary nutritionist is essential in order to determine the specific dietary requirements of your dog and achieve the necessary balance. Factors such as age, breed, size, activity level, and any existing health conditions should be considered when formulating a balanced diet. Commercially available dog foods that meet the Association of American Feed Control Officials (AAFCO) standards can also provide a reliable source of balanced nutrition for your dog.

Remember that maintaining the correct balance of macronutrients and micronutrients is essential for your dog's overall health and well-being. A properly balanced diet will support their growth, development, immune system function, energy levels, and longevity. By consistently keeping track of your dog's body condition, weight, and general health, and making necessary adjustments to their diet, you can ensure they receive the ideal nutrition required for their well-being and growth.

CALCULATING PORTION SIZES

Calculating portion sizes for proper balance in your dog's diet is an essential aspect of ensuring their nutritional needs are met. When figuring out the right quantity of food to give your dog, you need to consider multiple factors.

- Dog's Size and Weight: The size and weight of your dog play a significant role in determining portion sizes. Larger dogs generally require more food compared to smaller breeds. Referring to the feeding guidelines offered by the dog food manufacturer is crucial as a foundational reference.

- Age and Activity Level: Puppies and active dogs have higher energy requirements than adult or less active dogs. Growing puppies need more food to support their development, while highly active dogs may require additional calories to fuel their activities. Adjusting portion sizes based on age and activity level is crucial to prevent under or overfeeding.

- Dog Food Type: Different types of dog food, such as kibble, wet food, or raw diets, have varying nutrient densities. Adhere to the suggested feeding instructions indicated on the packaging, or seek advice from a veterinarian to ascertain the suitable portion sizes depending on the particular food you are utilizing.

- Calorie Content: Understanding the calorie content of your dog's food is crucial in calculating portion sizes accurately. Dog food labels typically provide information on the number of calories per cup or per serving. You can use this information to calculate the appropriate daily caloric intake for your dog.

- Body Condition Score: Evaluating your dog's body condition score can help determine if they are at an ideal weight or if adjustments need to be made to their portion sizes. A veterinarian can assist in assessing your dog's body condition score and provide guidance on adjusting portion sizes accordingly.

Feeding: First Year Timeline

Dog's Age	Feeding Guidelines
2-3 months	Puppies between the age of 2 months and 3 months should always be fed specialized puppy food to meet the needs for normal development. If you feed your puppy adult dog food, it will not provide the puppy with the necessary nutrients for good health. At this age, your pup should be fed four times a day to meet its nutritional demands. Bigger breeds should start to be fed unmoistened dry food by between month two and three, and for small dogs at month 3.
3-6 months	During this period, it is safe to decrease your feedings from four times a day to three times a day. Your pup should be losing its belly and chubbiness by month three. If your pup is still quite chubby and pudgy, continue to feed him/her puppy-sized portions till his/her body matures.
6-12 months	When your puppy reaches 6 months of age, you can decrease your feeding from three times a day to twice a day. This is around the time that you should be getting your dog spayed/neutered. Spaying and neutering lower the energy requirements of your pup and this is when it is okay to switch from the nutrient-rich puppy food to adult dog food that maintains the nutrients. Smaller breeds can switch between month seven and month nine. Larger breeds typically switch at the one-year mark. When in doubt, it is better to be on puppy food longer than less.

12 months +	At the age of one, most dog owners are recommended to continue feeding their dog twice a day but at half portions (1/2 portion total per day) but this is dependent on breed and metabolism.

So how much food should I be giving my puppy? The answer is complicated as portion sizes depend entirely on the dog's individual metabolism and body type. Nutritional value varies from dog to dog just like humans. If your puppy occasionally misses a meal, you don't have to worry. It may mean that your pup is ready to have fewer feedings a day.

Every day, your dog should consume roughly 2.5 percent of his body weight, according to a typical rule. You'll increase or decrease this depending on your dog's activity level and whether you're attempting to maintain, lose weight, or gain weight.

Below is a generic puppy feeding chart that you can follow. You can determine how many cups you should be feeding your pup based on its age in months and its weight in pounds (lbs).

Generic Dog Feeding Chart

Weight of Dog	Age: 1 – 3 months	Age: 4 – 5 months	Age: 6 – 8 months	Age: 9 – 11 months	Age: 1 – 2 years
(LBS)	Cup(s) per Day	Cup(s) per Day	Cup(s) per Day	Cup(s) per Day	Cup(s) per Day
3 - 12	0.5 - 1	0.6 - 1.25	0.5 - 1.5	Feed as an adult dog	Feed as an adult dog
13 - 20	0.5 - 1.25	1.2 - 2	0.75 - 1.3	1 - 1.5	Feed as an adult dog
21 - 50	0.5 - 1.5	1.5 - 2.6	1.2 - 2.3	2 - 3	2 - 4.25
51 - 75	0.6 - 2.25	1.5 - 4	1.5 - 3.75	2.5 - 4.75	2.6 - 6.25
76 - 100	1 - 2.5	2.75 - 3.75	2.75 - 6.3	3.75 - 7	5.6 - 11
101 +	2.5 + 0.3 cups for every 10 lbs. of body weight over 100 lbs.	3.75 cups + 0.3 cups for every 10lb of body weight over 100 lbs.	6.3 cups + 0.3 cups for every 10 lbs. of body weight over 100 lbs.	7 cups + 0.3 cups for every 10 lbs. of body weight over 100 lbs.	11 cups + 0.3 cups for every 10 lbs. of body weight over 100 lbs.

CALCULATING CALORIC NEEDS

The type, amount and frequency of calories your dog consumes is determined by many factors, including his or her size and metabolism. Obesity may result from overfeeding your dog with extra energy. This can result in a variety of health problems. As a result, your dog's health requires that he or she get the correct quantity of appropriate food. A formula has been established by veterinarians to estimate the calorie requirements of your dog.

(Body weight of your dog in kilograms x 30) + 70 = RER *

* RER: The calculated value gives the calorie requirement per day without any activity.

To measure other factors are also essential for the actual calorie requirement, the RER is multiplied by a factor that takes your dog's living situation into account:

- Adult, normally active dog, neutered: 1.6 x RER

- Adult, normally active dog, not neutered: 1.8 x RER

- Your dog does light work: 2 x RER

- Your dog does moderate work: 3 x RER

- Your dog does heavy work: 4-8 x RER

- Your dog is pregnant (<42 days): 1.8 x RER

- Your dog is pregnant (three weeks prior to the birth): 3 x RER

- Your dog is suckling puppies: 4-8 x RER (depending on how many puppies need to be looked after)

- Your puppy is younger than four months: 3 x RER

- Your dog is older than 4 months but not yet an adult: 2 x RER

- Your dog should lose weight: 1 x RER

As an example, let us calculate the caloric needs of a five-year-old mixed breed, 13 kilograms, neutered.
13 kg x30 + 70 = 460 calories (RER)
460 x 1.6 RER = 736 calories per day

According to this calculation, the dog should be consuming 736 calories per day. To meet his demands, we must first know how many calories are in the daily diet.

Note: If you have the weight in pounds, divide it to 2.2 to get the weight in kilograms.
Once you have the total daily calories, you can divide it into meals based on your feeding schedule.

HOW TO MODIFY RECIPES TO MEET YOUR DOG'S NEEDS

Modifying recipes to meet your dog's needs is a great way to ensure they are getting a balanced & nutritious diet. Below are some steps to follow when making modifications:

1. Consult with a Veterinarian: Prior to making any alterations to your canine companion's food regimen, it is crucial to seek advice from a veterinarian. This professional can offer personalized recommendations considering your dog's individual requirements, including potential allergies, sensitivities, or existing health conditions.

2. Choose High-Quality Ingredients: Selecting high-quality ingredients is essential for your dog's health. Opt for lean proteins like chicken, turkey, or fish, and include a variety of vegetables and fruits that are safe for dogs. Steer clear of ingredients that can be harmful to dogs, like chocolate, onions, garlic, grapes, or raisins.

3. Adjust Portion Sizes: When modifying a recipe, consider the portion sizes based on your dog's size, weight, and activity level. Larger dogs will require more food, while smaller breeds or less active dogs may need smaller portions.

4. Balance Macronutrients: Dogs require a balanced diet that includes proteins, carbohydrates, and fats. Adjust the recipe's ingredients to ensure the appropriate balance. Protein should make up a significant portion of the diet, while carbohydrates and fats should be provided in moderation.

5. Avoid Seasonings and Additives: Many seasonings and additives used in human recipes can be harmful to dogs. Avoid using ingredients like salt, spices, artificial sweeteners, and preservatives. Stick to simple and natural ingredients to keep the recipe safe and healthy for your dog.

6. Cook Appropriately: When preparing homemade meals for your dog, ensure that ingredients are cooked thoroughly to eliminate any harmful bacteria. Avoid using excessive oils or fats when cooking, as they can lead to weight gain and other health issues.

7. Monitor & Adjust: Keep a close eye on your dog's reaction to the modified recipe to ensure they adapt well to the new diet. Keep an eye on their weight, energy levels, coat condition, and overall health. If necessary, adjust the recipe or consult with your veterinarian for further guidance.

BEST PRACTICES FOR STORING AND SERVING

HOMEMADE DOG FOOD

SAFE FOOD HANDLING PRACTICES

Safe food handling practices are crucial when preparing homemade dog food to ensure your dog's health and prevent foodborne illnesses. Here are some guidelines to follow:

1. Start by thoroughly washing your hands with soap and water prior to handling any ingredients or preparing the dog food. Make sure all utensils, cutting boards, and preparation surfaces are clean and sanitized.

2. Designate separate utensils and cutting boards for your dog's food preparation to avoid cross-contamination with human food. This helps prevent the transfer of harmful bacteria.

3. Use fresh ingredients when preparing homemade dog food. Avoid using expired or spoiled ingredients as they can lead to foodborne illnesses.

4. Store ingredients properly to maintain their freshness and prevent bacterial growth. Keep raw meats, poultry, and fish separate from other ingredients, and store them in sealed containers in the refrigerator or freezer.

5. Ensure that all animal proteins, such as meats, poultry, and fish, are cooked thoroughly to eliminate any harmful bacteria. Undercooked or raw meat can pose health risks to your dog.

6. Let cooked dog food to cool prior to transferring it to the refrigerator. Split the food into appropriate portions and store them in airtight containers. Refrigerate promptly to prevent bacterial growth.

7. Some ingredients that are safe for humans can be toxic or harmful to dogs. Avoid using ingredients such as chocolate, onions, garlic, grapes, raisins, avocados, and artificial sweeteners (like xylitol) as they can be toxic to dogs.

8. Serve homemade dog food to your dog within a reasonable time frame. To prevent bacterial growth, refrain from leaving it at room temperature for prolonged periods.

9. Regularly monitor the freshness of homemade dog food. If you observe any indications of food spoilage, like an unpleasant odor or unusual visual characteristics, dispose of the food right away.

10. When introducing homemade dog food into your dog's diet, do it gradually to avoid digestive issues. Begin by combining a small amount of the food arranged at home with their usual store-bought dog food, progressively increasing the proportion over the course of a few days.

By following these safe food handling practices, you can ensure that the homemade dog food you prepare is safe, healthy, and free from harmful bacteria, reducing the risk of foodborne illnesses for your furry friend.

TIPS FOR STORING HOMEMADE DOG FOOD

It is important to store your dog food in a manner which will maintain its quality and ensure its integrity is not contaminated. It is recommended to store it at temps that are not too hot or cold in sealed containers. Consider the following tips and tricks when storing all types of dog food so you'll always have a good source of food for your dog.

DRY DOG FOOD STORAGE

This is a great option for serving throughout the day and it doesn't spoil right away. Dogs enjoy crunching on fresh kibble, but an open bag can easily go stale or rancid if stored improperly. Consider the following tips to storing dry dog food:

Dry kibble should be stored in a sealed container made of plastic, glass, or aluminum. The original bag should be kept inside the container.

Select containers for storing pet food which have a rubber gasket, as this will help to prevent air and moisture from getting in. The food stored in these containers are going to be protected against contamination by air, moisture, and vermin.

Adding an extra layer of protection to the food by retaining it in its original packaging ensures that it will continue to taste nice. Additionally, it keeps the food from taking on the flavor of the container that it was stored in.

Because of the risk of temp. swings and the presence of unwanted pests like flies, mice, and different animals, food ought not be kept in an outdoor location. Food should ideally be stored indoors at a temperature of 71 degrees Fahrenheit (22°C) or less.

For maximum taste and freshness, you should use a bag of dry food within six weeks and always check the "best by" date to ensure it is still good.

CANNED DOG FOOD STORAGE

A lot of dogs prefer canned food since it is moist, meat-filled and often has a great texture and taste. If properly stored, canned food can last for years. There are a few precautions you can take to make sure the food stays safe and tasty when you give it to your dog:

Always check the "best by" date on the bottom to make sure the food isn't expired.

Check the cans for dents, swelling and/or punctures that could indicate spoilage or botulism.

Discard any cans that are suspect. When discarding suspect cans you should wrap the can in plastic and discard it in the trash. Wash your hands entirely or use disposable gloves when handling.

Pet food cans should be stored indoors at temperatures of 71 degrees Fahrenheit (22°C) or less. Unopened cans don't have to be refrigerated and most dogs prefer canned food that is at room temperature.

Dogs can have access to dry kibble throughout the day, but canned food shouldn't be left out at room temp. for an extended period of time because it can go bad. When you leave out kibble, you should only leave out enough for a 24-hour period. For canned food, you should allow it to sit out for more than four hours to avoid spoilage.

The flavor of any leftover moist food ought to be preserved by keeping it in its original can and covering it with a lid or plastic wrap. You are able to move it to a glass container that has a tight-fitting lid. The shelf life of any leftover canned food that has been stored is four days. Instead of storing it in the refrigerator, you may make it last further by wrapping individual servings in plastic wrap and freezing them for a maximum of three months.

STORING HOMEMADE FOOD

While preparing your own meal for your dog, the meat ought to attain an internal temp. of 165°F (75 degrees Celsius) before serving. This will ensure that the meat is thoroughly cooked. When you have a new batch ready to go, you can either put it into the fridge for approximately four days or freeze it for at least six months in a zippered bag or sealed container. When giving your dog fresh food, you should use the same level of caution that you would with food that comes in a can.

DOG TREATS

So long as they are not stale and have a pleasant flavor, treats are an excellent method to show affection for your pet. In order to accomplish this, please follow these steps:

Packages of sweets that have been opened but are still stored in their original packaging inside of a sealed container or a plastic bag that can be sealed again.

Treats ought to be maintained in temps below 71 °F (22 degrees Celsius).

The majority of candies are packaged in resealable bags to ensure that they maintain their freshness. This is particularly critical for treats that are soft in consistency.

If you have freshly baked cookies, put them in a bag or container that can be sealed again and put them in the fridge so that they stay as fresh as possible.

RAW DIET STORAGE

If you choose to offer a raw diet to your pet, there are some extra precautions you need to take when preserving their food. At room temp., raw meat can quickly become rancid. Raw foods should be stored in the fridge for no more than four days at a time in an airtight container.

When preparing food in large quantities, it is best to keep it in the freezer using freezer-safe containers or resealable plastic bags. If it is protected against freezer burn, food that has been frozen can be edible for a maximum of six months.

Consumption of raw food must take place in a single sitting. The leftovers need to be collected right away and placed in the fridge for safekeeping. When left out at room temp. for longer than two hours, raw meat poses a health risk.

Due to the increased probability that it may go bad, raw meat ought not to be provided in time feeders. After touching any kind of raw meat, you ought to make sure to properly wash your hands.

TIPS ON HOW TO MANAGE HOMEMADE DOG FOOD PORTIONS

Storing and using portions of homemade dog food after it has been cooked requires proper handling to maintain freshness and prevent bacterial growth. Here are some tips to help you store and use homemade dog food effectively:

- Use portioning tools: Investing in portioning tools can help ensure accuracy and consistency in serving sizes. Measuring cups or scoops specifically designed for pet food can help you measure out the correct amount of food for each portion.

- Labeling: Label each portion with the date of preparation and the contents. This ensures that you can easily identify and track the freshness of each batch. It's best to use the oldest portions first to prevent spoilage.

- Refrigeration: If you plan to use the portions within a few days, store them in the refrigerator. Keep the dog food refrigerated at or below 40°F (4°C) to prevent bacterial growth. Use a dedicated shelf or section of the refrigerator to avoid cross-contamination with human food.

- Freezing: If you want to store the dog food for a more extended period, freezing is an excellent option. Freezing helps preserve the freshness and nutritional value of the food. Place the portions in freezer-safe containers or bags, remove extra air, and seal them tightly. Freeze the portions at 0°F (-18°C) or below.

- Thawing: When it's time to use a portion of frozen dog food, transfer it from the freezer to the refrigerator the night prior to to thaw slowly. Thawing in the refrigerator helps maintain food safety. Alternatively, you can thaw the portion in a microwave or under cool running water, but be sure to use it immediately.

- Avoid refreezing: Once a portion of homemade dog food has been thawed, it's best to use it within 2-3 days. Avoid refreezing previously thawed portions, as this can affect the quality and safety of the food.

- Hygiene and food safety: Practice good hygiene when handling and serving homemade dog food. Wash your hands prior to and after handling the food. Use clean utensils and containers to prevent contamination. Discard any uneaten portions that have been left out at room temperature for more than two hours.

- Monitor freshness: Pay attention to the smell, appearance, and texture of the stored dog food. If you notice any signs of spoilage, such as an off odor, mold, or unusual color, discard the portion immediately.

TRANSITIONING YOUR DOG TO A HOMEMADE DIET

HOW TO INTRODUCE NEW FOOD GRADUALLY

Introducing new food gradually is essential when transitioning your dog to a homemade dog food diet. A gradual transition helps prevent digestive upset and allows your dog's system to adjust to the new diet. Here's a step-by-step guide to introducing new food gradually:

1. Start with Small Amounts: Begin by mixing a small amount of the homemade dog food with your dog's current commercial dog food. Initially, the proportion of homemade food should be small, around 10-25% of the total meal.

2. Monitor Digestive Response: Monitor your dog's reaction to the new food in the upcoming days. Keep an eye out for any indications of digestive discomfort, such as diarrhea, throwing up, or reduced appetite. If your dog shows any negative responses, seek advice from your veterinarian.

3. Increase Proportion Gradually: Gradually increase the proportion of homemade dog food in each meal while reducing the amount of commercial food. Aim to make the transition over the course of about one to two weeks, depending on your dog's tolerance and sensitivity.

4. Monitor for Transition Issues: Continue monitoring your dog's digestion and overall well-being throughout the transition period. If you notice any persistent digestive issues, slow down the transition process or seek guidance from your veterinarian.

5. Maintain Consistency: Ensure consistency in the ingredients and preparation of the homemade dog food throughout the transition period. This consistency helps your dog's digestive system adapt more easily.

6. Monitor Body Condition: Keep an eye on your dog's body condition during the transition process. Adjust the portion sizes of the new homemade food as needed to maintain a healthy weight. Your veterinarian can provide guidance on appropriate portion sizes.

7. Gradual Elimination of Commercial Food: Once your dog has successfully transitioned to the homemade dog food, you can gradually eliminate the commercial food entirely. However, it's essential to ensure that the homemade diet provides all the necessary nutrients for your dog's well-being.

Remember, each dog is unique, and the transition period may vary. Some dogs may adjust quickly, while others may require a slower transition. Always consult with your veterinarian for guidance tailored to your dog's specific needs. By gradually introducing the new homemade food, you can help ensure a uniform transition and promote your dog's overall health and well-being.

WHAT TO EXPECT DURING THE TRANSITION PERIOD

During the transition period to a new homemade dog food diet, it's essential to be aware of certain changes and expectations. Here's what you can expect during this transition period:

Digestive Changes: Some dogs may experience mild digestive changes during the transition. This can include softer stools or occasional gastrointestinal upset such as gas or mild diarrhea. These changes are often temporary and should resolve as your dog's system adjusts to the new diet. If the digestive issues persist or worsen, consult with your veterinarian.

Change in Appetite: Your dog's appetite may fluctuate during the transition period. Some dogs may show increased interest in the new food, while others may initially be hesitant. As long as your dog is maintaining a healthy weight and overall well-being, minor fluctuations in appetite are usually normal. However, consult with your veterinarian if your dog's appetite significantly decreases or if they refuse to eat.

Gradual Adjustment: Dogs generally benefit from a gradual transition to minimize the chances of digestive upset. It may take anywhere from a few days to a couple of weeks for your dog to fully adjust to the new diet. Be patient and monitor your dog's response throughout the transition.

Increased Water Intake: Switching to a new diet, particularly one that contains higher moisture content, such as homemade dog food, may result in increased water intake. This is generally a positive change as it helps maintain proper hydration and supports healthy digestion. Ensure that fresh water is always available for your dog.

Coat and Skin Changes: A change in diet can sometimes lead to changes in your dog's coat and skin. You may notice improvements in coat quality, such as increased shine or softness. Conversely, some dogs may experience temporary dryness or minor skin reactions during the transition. If skin issues persist or worsen, consult with your veterinarian.

Energy and Behavior: As your dog adjusts to the new diet, you may notice changes in their energy levels and behavior. Some dogs may experience increased energy and improved overall vitality, while others may take time to adapt. Monitor these changes and consult with your veterinarian if you have concerns about significant behavioral shifts.

Regular Monitoring: Throughout the transition period, it's essential to monitor your dog's body condition, weight, and overall health. Keep an eye on their appetite, digestion, energy levels, coat condition, and any other relevant factors. Regular communication with your veterinarian will help address any issues and ensure a uniform transition.

Remember, every dog is unique, and the transition period can vary. If you have any concerns or if your dog's symptoms persist or worsen during the transition, consult with your veterinarian. They can provide specific guidance based on your dog's individual needs and help ensure a successful transition to the new homemade dog food diet.

MANAGING SPECIFIC DIETARY REQUIREMENTS

OR ALLERGIES

HOW TO PREPARE HOMEMADE DOG FOOD FOR DOGS WITH ALLERGIES

When preparing homemade dog food for dogs with allergies, it's essential to identify and avoid the specific allergens causing the reaction. Below are some steps to help you prepare homemade dog food for dogs with allergies:

Identify Allergens: Work with your veterinarian to identify the specific allergens causing your dog's allergic reactions. This may involve conducting allergy tests or performing elimination diets to pinpoint the problematic ingredients.

Eliminate Allergenic Ingredients: Once you have identified the allergens, eliminate them from your dog's diet entirely. Common allergens for dogs include beef, chicken, dairy, wheat, soy, and certain grains. Eliminate these ingredients from your homemade dog food recipes.

Choose Hypoallergenic Ingredients: Select hypoallergenic ingredients to use in your homemade dog food. These are ingredients that are less likely to cause allergic reactions. Examples include novel protein sources like venison, rabbit, duck, or fish, and carbohydrates like sweet potatoes, quinoa, or rice. Seek guidance from your veterinarian to receive personalized recommendations tailored to your dog's allergies.

Recipe Development: Develop homemade dog food recipes using the hypoallergenic ingredients you have chosen. Ensure that the recipes provide a balanced and complete diet that meets your dog's nutritional needs. It's recommended to work with a veterinary nutritionist or consult with your veterinarian to create a well-balanced recipe.

Cook Thoroughly: Cook all ingredients thoroughly to eliminate any potential allergens and to ensure the food is safe for consumption. Avoid using excessive oils or fats in the cooking process, as they can lead to weight gain or digestive issues.

Gradual Introduction: Introduce the new homemade dog food gradually to allow your dog's system to adjust. Start by mixing a small portion of the homemade food with their current diet, gradually increasing the proportion of the homemade food over time.

Monitor for Improvement: Keep a close eye on your dog's response to the new homemade food. Monitor for any signs of improvement in their allergic symptoms, such as reduced itching, skin irritations, or digestive issues. If you notice positive changes, it indicates that the new diet may be better suited to your dog's allergies.

Regular Check-ups: Make it a habit to set up regular appointments with your vet to evaluate your dog's development and guarantee their dietary requirements are being fulfilled. Your veterinarian can provide guidance on monitoring your dog's allergies and adjusting the homemade diet as necessary.

It's essential to note that homemade dog food diets, especially for dogs with allergies, should be formulated with care to provide a balanced and complete nutritional profile. Consider consulting with a veterinary nutritionist or seeking professional guidance to ensure that your homemade dog food meets your dog's specific dietary needs.

DOGS WITH SPECIFIC DIETARY NEEDS

Dogs with specific dietary needs require special attention to ensure they receive the proper nutrition. Here are some common dietary needs and guidelines for addressing them:

Weight Management: If your dog needs to lose or maintain weight, it's essential to provide portion-controlled meals that are balanced in nutrients. Work with your veterinarian to determine the appropriate calorie intake for your dog's weight loss or maintenance goals. Consider incorporating lean proteins, healthy fats, and high-fiber ingredients to help your dog feel satisfied. Avoid excessive treats and monitor their overall calorie intake.

Food Allergies or Sensitivities: Dogs with food allergies or sensitivities require a carefully planned diet that avoids triggering ingredients. Identify the allergens through allergy tests or elimination diets, and eliminate those ingredients from your dog's diet. Replace them with alternative protein and carbohydrate sources that your dog can tolerate. Consult with a veterinary nutritionist to ensure the diet remains balanced and provides all necessary nutrients.

Digestive Issues: Dogs with digestive issues may benefit from a diet that is easily digestible and gentle on the stomach. Consider providing meals that include highly digestible proteins, such as lean meats or novel protein sources. Avoid ingredients that commonly cause gastrointestinal upset, such as grains or certain fiber sources. Probiotics or digestive enzymes may also be beneficial in some cases.

Renal or Liver Disease: Dogs with renal or liver disease require a special diet to support their organ function and manage their condition. These diets are typically lower in protein, phosphorus, and sodium. Work with your veterinarian to select commercial renal or liver-supportive diets or consult with a veterinary nutritionist to formulate a homemade diet that meets your dog's specific needs.

Dental Health: For dogs with dental issues, it may be necessary to modify the texture of their food. Softer or wet food options can be easier for them to chew and swallow. You can also incorporate dental treats or provide dental chews approved by your veterinarian to help maintain their oral health.

Senior Dogs: Senior dogs may benefit from diets that address age-related issues, such as joint health or cognitive function. Look for senior-specific commercial diets that include ingredients like glucosamine, chondroitin, and antioxidants. These ingredients can help support joint health and brain function in older dogs.

It is essential to consistently seek advice from your veterinarian in order to establish the most suitable approach for addressing your dog's unique dietary requirements. Your veterinarian can offer guidance, suggest suitable commercial diets, or collaborate with you to develop a homemade diet that fulfills your dog's needs. Regular monitoring and check-ups are crucial to ensure your dog's dietary needs are adequately addressed and to make any necessary modifications as needed.

FREQUENTLY ASKED QUESTIONS ABOUT

HOMEMADE DOG FOOD

IS HOMEMADE DOG FOOD BETTER THAN COMMERCIAL DOG FOOD?

Homemade dog food can be a good option if formulated properly with a veterinarian's guidance. It allows for better control over ingredients and can be tailored to a dog's specific dietary needs.

CAN I FEED MY DOG ONLY MEAT AND BONES?

No, a diet solely composed of meat and bones is not nutritionally balanced for dogs. They require a variety of nutrients from different food groups to thrive.

CAN I FEED MY DOG RAW FOOD?

Yes, you can feed your dog raw food. Feeding a raw food diet is a personal choice that some dog owners opt for. It typically consists of uncooked meat, bones, organs, fruits, and vegetables. Proponents of raw feeding believe that it can provide various benefits, including improved digestion, healthier skin and coat, increased energy levels, and dental health support.

However, it is essential to note that feeding a raw diet carries certain risks. Raw meat can potentially contain harmful bacteria like Salmonella or E. coli, which can pose health risks to both dogs and their owners. Proper handling, storage, and hygiene practices are crucial to minimize the risk of bacterial contamination. Additionally, ensuring a nutritionally balanced raw diet can be challenging without expert guidance or pre-made balanced raw food products.

HOW CAN I ENSURE MY HOMEMADE DOG FOOD IS NUTRITIONALLY BALANCED?

To ensure your homemade dog food is nutritionally balanced, it is crucial to consult with a veterinarian or veterinary nutritionist who can provide expert guidance. They can help you understand your dog's specific nutritional requirements, create a balanced meal plan, and recommend appropriate supplements if needed. Utilize reliable recipes or work with a professional to develop a customized recipe that includes essential nutrients such as proteins, carbohydrates, fats, vitamins, and minerals. Select high-quality ingredients, including lean meats or plant-based proteins, fruits, vegetables, and whole grains. Regularly monitor your dog's body condition, overall health, and energy levels, and make necessary adjustments to the diet under the guidance of your veterinarian. By following these steps and seeking professional advice, you can ensure that your homemade dog food provides the necessary nutrition for your furry friend's well-being.

CAN I USE LEFTOVERS FROM MY OWN MEALS AS DOG FOOD?

It's generally not recommended to feed dogs leftovers from your own meals regularly. Many human foods contain spices, seasonings, or ingredients that may be harmful to dogs. Additionally, leftovers may not provide the balanced nutrition that dogs need.

CAN I SWITCH MY DOG TO HOMEMADE FOOD WITHOUT A GRADUAL TRANSITION?

No, it is generally not recommended to switch your dog to homemade food without a gradual transition. Sudden dietary changes can cause digestive upset, including diarrhea or vomiting. To avoid these issues, it is best to gradually introduce the homemade food by mixing it with the current commercial dog food over a period of 7 to 10 days, gradually increasing the proportion of homemade food.

CAN I FREEZE HOMEMADE DOG FOOD?

Yes, homemade dog food can be frozen in portion-sized containers for convenience. Freezing can help preserve the food's freshness and nutritional value.

HOW LONG CAN HOMEMADE DOG FOOD BE STORED IN THE REFRIGERATOR?

Homemade dog food should be stored in the refrigerator and used within 3-5 days to ensure freshness and minimize the risk of bacterial growth.

ARE THERE ANY RISKS OR DRAWBACKS TO FEEDING HOMEMADE DOG FOOD?

Feeding homemade dog food can have various risks and drawbacks that should be considered. One significant concern is the potential for nutritional imbalances. Dogs have specific dietary requirements, and without proper knowledge or guidance, homemade diets can lack essential nutrients, leading to deficiencies or excesses. This can have detrimental effects on the dog's overall health and well-being.

Another drawback is the time and effort involved in preparing homemade dog food. It can be a time-consuming process that requires research, recipe selection, ingredient sourcing, and meal preparation. This can be challenging for busy pet owners or those lacking culinary skills.

Food safety is another concern. Handling raw meats and other ingredients requires proper hygiene practices to avoid bacterial contamination. Without careful attention to food handling and storage, there is a risk of foodborne illnesses for both dogs and humans.

CAN I SUBSTITUTE GRAINS WITH OTHER CARBOHYDRATES IN HOMEMADE DOG FOOD?

Yes, if your dog has a grain sensitivity or you prefer to avoid grains, you can substitute them with other carbohydrate sources like sweet potatoes, quinoa, or legumes. Ensure the replacements are cooked properly to improve digestibility.

CAN I FEED MY DOG A VEGETARIAN OR VEGAN HOMEMADE DIET?

Feeding a dog a vegetarian or vegan homemade diet is possible, but it requires careful consideration and expert guidance to ensure that the dog's nutritional needs are met. Dogs are naturally omnivorous, meaning they can consume and digest both meat and plant-based foods.

ARE THERE ANY PRECAUTIONS I SHOULD TAKE WHEN HANDLING AND STORING HOMEMADE DOG FOOD?

Ensuring appropriate food safety measures while handling and storing homemade dog food is crucial. Prioritize washing your hands meticulously prior to and after food preparation, employ sanitized utensils and surfaces, and store the food in airtight containers within the refrigerator or freezer to hinder the growth of bacteria.

DO I NEED TO MONITOR MY DOG'S WEIGHT WHEN FEEDING HOMEMADE DOG FOOD?

Yes, it's essential to monitor your dog's weight when feeding homemade dog food, just as you would with any other type of diet. Dogs, like humans, can gain or lose weight depending on their caloric intake and activity level. It's essential to adjust the portion sizes and ingredients in the homemade diet to maintain a healthy weight for your dog. Regularly assess your dog's body condition and consult with a veterinarian if you have concerns about their weight.

CAN I USE ORGANIC INGREDIENTS IN HOMEMADE DOG FOOD?

Yes, you can use organic ingredients in homemade dog food if you prefer. Organic ingredients are produced without the use of synthetic fertilizers, pesticides, or genetically modified organisms (GMOs). However, it's essential to note that organic ingredients alone do not guarantee a nutritionally balanced diet. It is still necessary to ensure that the homemade dog food recipe contains all the essential nutrients your dog requires.

BREAKFAST AND DINNER RECIPES

Chicken and Veggie Omelet

Preparation time: 12 minutes

Cooking time: 16 minutes

Servings: 4

Ingredients:

- 4 eggs (whisked)
- 1 cup cooked chicken (shredded)
- 1/2 cup bell peppers (diced)
- 1/2 cup zucchini (diced)
- 1/2 cup broccoli (severed)

Directions:

1. In a non-stick griddle, sauté the bell peppers, zucchini, and broccoli till mildly tender.

2. Pour the whisked eggs over the sautéed vegetables and cook till set.

3. Flip the omelet and include the ragged chicken. Cook for another minute.

4. Cut the omelet into four portions and serve.

Tuna and Brown Rice Surprise

Preparation time: 6 minutes

Cooking time: 18 minutes

Servings: 2

Ingredients:

- 1 can tuna in water (drained)
- 1/2 cup cooked brown rice
- 1/4 cup spinach (severed)
- 1/8 cup carrots (grated)
- 1/2 tbsp flaxseed oil

Directions:

1. Inside your mixing container, blend the drained tuna, cooked brown rice, severed spinach, and grated carrots.

2. Drizzle flaxseed oil over the solution and mix well.

3. Serve the tuna and brown rice solution in individual portions.

Lamb and Rice Pilaf

Preparation time: 8 minutes

Cooking time: 36 minutes

Servings: 2

Ingredients:

- 1/2 cup cooked ground lamb
- 1/2 cup cooked rice
- 1/4 cup green peas
- 1/8 cup carrots (diced)
- 1/2 tbsp canola oil

Directions:

1. Inside a griddle, warm the canola oil across moderate flame.

2. Include the ground lamb, cooked rice, green peas, and diced carrots. Stir-fry for five to seven mins, or till heated through.

3. Let the pilaf to cool mildly prior to serving.

Raw Breakfast

Preparation time: 6 minutes

Cooking time: -

Servings: 1

Ingredients:

- 1 frozen raw veggie cupcake (thawed)
- one teaspoon flaxseed oil
- 1/2 teaspoon raw honey
- 1 egg
- 2 tbsps plain yogurt or cottage cheese
- 1/2 teaspoon of organic apple cider vinegar
- 1-ounce heart meat
- 1 chicken liver (rinsed)

Directions:

1. Cautiously crack your egg into a mixing container and grind the eggshell into fine small pieces.

2. Include your chicken liver along with the heart meat, then stir in the honey, yogurt, flaxseed oil, apple cider vinegar.

3. Serve along with thawed Raw Veggie Cupcake for a full breakfast for your furry pal!

Veggie Egg Scramble

Preparation time: 11 minutes

Cooking time: 8 minutes

Servings: 4

Ingredients:

- 8 eggs (whisked)
- 1/2 cup bell peppers (diced)
- 1/2 cup spinach (severed)
- 2 tbsp olive oil

Directions:

1. Warm the olive oil in your non-stick griddle across moderate flame.

2. Include the diced bell peppers, and severed spinach to the griddle. Sauté for two to three mins till the vegetables are mildly tender.

3. Pour the whisked eggs over the vegetables and cook, mixing gently, till the eggs are scrambled and cooked through.

4. Split the scrambled eggs into four portions and serve.

Pork and Barley Stew

Preparation time: 14 minutes

Cooking time: 46 minutes

Servings: 3

Ingredients:

- 1/2 lb. pork loin (cubed)
- 1/2 cup barley (cooked)
- 1/4 cup green beans (severed)
- 1/4 cup carrots (diced)
- 1 cup low-sodium chicken broth

Directions:

1. Inside a big pot, brown the pork loin cubes across moderate flame. Drain extra fat.

2. Include the cooked barley, severed green beans, diced carrots, and chicken broth to the pot.

3. Boil, then diminish heat then simmer for forty mins or 'til the pork is cooked through and soft.

4. Let the stew to cool prior to serving.

Turkey Meatballs with Vegetables

Preparation time: 14 minutes

Cooking time: 20-25 minutes

Servings: 4

Ingredients:

- 1 lb. ground turkey
- 1/2 cup breadcrumbs
- 1/4 cup grated carrots
- 1/4 cup grated zucchini
- 1/4 cup severed parsley

Directions:

1. Warm up the oven to 375 deg. F.
2. Inside a container, blend the ground turkey, breadcrumbs, grated carrots, grated zucchini, and severed parsley. Mix thoroughly.
3. Shape the solution into small meatballs then put them on a baking surface lined with parchment paper.
4. Bake for twenty to twenty-five mins, or 'til the meatballs are cooked through.
5. Let the meatballs to cool prior to serving.

Turkey and Quinoa Medley

Preparation time: 12 minutes

Cooking time: 18 minutes

Servings: 2

Ingredients:

- 1/2 cup cooked ground turkey
- 1/4 cup cooked quinoa
- 1/8 cup peas
- 1/8 cup carrots (diced)
- 1/2 tbsp coconut oil

Directions:

1. Inside a griddle, warm the coconut oil across moderate flame.
2. Include the ground turkey, quinoa, peas, and carrots to the griddle. Cook for five to seven mins, or 'til heated through.
3. Eliminate from flame then let it cool mildly prior to serving.

Chicken and Pumpkin Stew

Preparation time: 15 minutes

Cooking time: 38 minutes

Servings: 3

Ingredients:

- 1 cup cooked chicken (shredded)
- 1/2 cup pumpkin puree
- 1/4 cup peas
- 1/4 cup carrots (diced)
- 1 cup low-sodium chicken broth

Directions:

1. Inside a pot, blend the shredded chicken, pumpkin puree, peas, diced carrots, and chicken broth.

2. Boil, then diminish flame then simmer for thirty mins or till the carrots are soft.

3. Let the stew to cool prior to serving.

Salmon and Sweet Potato Cakes

Preparation time: 18 minutes

Cooking time: 22 minutes

Servings: 3

Ingredients:

- 1/2 can salmon (drained and flaked)
- 1 sweet potato (cooked and mashed)
- 1/4 cup oats
- 1/2 egg (whisked)
- 1/8 cup parsley (severed)

Directions:

1. Inside a container, blend the salmon, mashed sweet potatoes, oats, whisked egg, and severed parsley. Mix thoroughly.

2. Form the solution into small patties.

3. Heat a non-stick griddle across moderate flame then cook the patties for three to four mins on each side, or till golden brown.

4. Let the cakes to cool prior to serving.

Beef and Potato Hash

Preparation time: 16 minutes

Cooking time: 28 minutes

Servings: 6

Ingredients:

- 1½ lbs ground beef
- 3 potatoes (cooked and diced)
- 3/4 cup green beans (severed)
- 1/3 cup carrots (diced)
- 1½ tbsps canola oil

Directions:

1. In your griddle, brown the ground beef across moderate flame. Drain extra fat.

2. Include the diced potatoes, severed green beans, diced carrots, and canola oil to the griddle. Sauté for ten-fifteen mins till the vegetables are soft.

3. Let the hash to cool prior to serving.

Fruits & Vegetables Breakfast

Preparation time: 16 minutes

Cooking time: -

Servings: 2

Ingredients:

- 2/3 cup vegetables (celery, broccoli, spinach, carrots, etc.)
- 2/3 cup fruits (apples etc.)
- 2/3 cup rolled oats
- 1 cup yogurt
- 2 tsp honey
- 2 tsp apple cider vinegar
- 2 tsp kelp seaweed powder (shredded and mildly steamed)
- 2 tsp alfalfa powder
- 2 tsp flax seed oil

Directions:

1. Immerse rolled oats in yogurt overnight.

2. Blend the entire components and serve.

Lentil and Vegetable Stew

Preparation time: 12 minutes

Cooking time: 38 minutes

Servings: 3

Ingredients:

- 1/2 cup cooked lentils
- 1/4 cup sweet potatoes (diced)
- 1/4 cup green beans (severed)
- 1/8 cup carrots (diced)
- 1 cup low-sodium vegetable broth

Directions:

1. In a pot, blend the cooked lentils, diced sweet potatoes, severed green beans, diced carrots, and vegetable broth.

2. Boil, afterwards diminish warm then simmer for thirty-forty mins or till the vegetables are soft.

3. Let the stew to cool prior to serving.

Fish and Rice Medley

Preparation time: 12 minutes

Cooking time: 32 minutes

Servings: 2

Ingredients:

- 1/2 lb. white fish fillets (cooked and flaked)
- 1/2 cup cooked rice
- 1/4 cup broccoli florets (steamed)
- 1/8 cup carrots (grated)
- 1/2 tbsp flaxseed oil

Directions:

1. Inside a container, blend the cooked and flaked fish, cooked rice, steamed broccoli florets, and grated carrots.

2. Drizzle flaxseed oil over the solution and mix well.

3. Serve the fish and rice medley in individual portions.

Filet Mignon with Sweet Potato Mash

Preparation time: 8 minutes

Cooking time: 18 minutes

Servings: 1

Ingredients:

- 1 filet mignon steak
- 1 sweet potato (cooked and mashed)
- 1/8 cup green beans (steamed)
- 1/8 cup carrots (steamed)
- 1/2 tbsp olive oil

Directions:

1. Warm up the grill or a griddle across moderate-high flame.

2. Rub the filet mignon steak with olive oil.

3. Cook the steak for 4-6 mins on every end, or till anticipated level of doneness.

4. Serve the filet mignon with the sweet potato mash, steamed green beans, and steamed carrots.

Salmon and Quinoa Salad

Preparation time: 12 minutes

Cooking time: 22 minutes

Servings: 2

Ingredients:

- 1 cup cooked salmon (flaked)
- 1/2 cup cooked quinoa
- 1/4 cup cherry tomatoes (halved)
- 1/8 cup cucumber (diced)
- 1 tbsp lemon juice

Directions:

1. Inside a container, blend the flaked salmon, cooked quinoa, halved cherry tomatoes, diced cucumber, and lemon juice. Toss gently to mix.

2. Serve the salmon and quinoa salad in individual portions.

Venison and Sweet Potato Stew

Preparation time: 10 minutes

Cooking time: 42 minutes

Servings: 3

Ingredients:

- 1 lb. venison (cubed)
- 1 sweet potato (skinned and diced)
- 1/4 cup peas
- 1/4 cup carrots (diced)
- 1 cup low-sodium beef or venison broth

Directions:

1. Inside a pot, brown the cubed venison across moderate flame. Drain extra fat.

2. Include the diced sweet potato, peas, carrots, and beef or venison broth to the pot.

3. Boil, then diminish flame then simmer for thirty-forty mins or till the venison is cooked through and soft.

4. Let the stew to cool prior to serving.

Beef and Sweet Potato Casserole

Preparation time: 16 minutes

Cooking time: 48 minutes

Servings: 6

Ingredients:

- 1 lb. ground beef
- 2 sweet potatoes (skinned and sliced)
- 1 cup peas
- 1 cup carrots (diced)
- 2 cups low-sodium beef broth

Directions:

1. Warm up the oven to 375 deg. F.

2. Inside your griddle, brown the ground beef across moderate flame. Drain extra fat.

3. Layer the sliced sweet potatoes, cooked ground beef, peas, and diced carrots in a baking dish.

4. Pour the beef broth across the casserole.

5. Close the baking dish with foil then bake for thirty to thirty-five mins. Take the foil then bake for an additional ten-fifteen mins 'til the sweet potatoes are soft.

6. Let the casserole to cool prior to serving.

Duck and Pumpkin Stew

Preparation time: 14 minutes

Cooking time: 40 minutes

Servings: 2

Ingredients:

- 1 cup cooked duck (shredded)
- 1/2 cup pumpkin puree
- 1/4 cup green peas
- 1/4 cup carrots (diced)
- 1 cup low-sodium duck or chicken broth

Directions:

1. In a pot, blend the shredded duck, pumpkin puree, green peas, diced carrots, and duck or chicken broth.

2. Boil, afterwards diminish flame then simmer for thirty mins or till the carrots are soft.

3. Let the stew to cool prior to serving.

Lamb and Quinoa Pilaf

Preparation time: 14 minutes

Cooking time: 34 minutes

Servings: 2

Ingredients:

- 1/2 cup cooked ground lamb
- 1/2 cup cooked quinoa
- 1/4 cup green peas
- 1/8 cup carrots (diced)
- 1/2 tbsp olive oil

Directions:

1. In your griddle, warm the olive oil across moderate flame.

2. Include the ground lamb, cooked quinoa, green peas, and diced carrots. Stir-fry for five to seven mins, or till heated through.

3. Let the pilaf to cool mildly prior to serving.

Weight Loss Chicken

Preparation time: 13 minutes

Cooking time: 20 minutes

Servings: 6-8 cups

Ingredients:

- 1 lb. minced chicken
- 2 cups rice
- 2 chicken stock cubes
- 1/2 cup frozen peas

Instructions:

1. Put the entire components into the big saucepan. Sprinkle the components an amount of water that is sufficient to cover all.

2. Cook across a moderate-high flame for about twenty mins, or till the rice has puffed up and the chicken is cooked all the way through.

3. Pour into a jar that can be sealed, and then store it in the refrigerator for around three days. To accompany, serve homemade kibble for dogs.

Raw Meat and Yoghurt

Preparation time: 14 minutes

Cooking time: -

Servings: 1

Ingredients:

- 3/4 oz raw meat
- 1 egg (raw)
- 1 tbsp yogurt
- 1/2 tsp honey
- 1/2 tbsp apple cider vinegar
- 1/4 tsp flax seed oil
- 1/2 tsp kelp seaweed powder
- 1/2 tsp alfalfa powder
- 1/8 cup kibble (optional)

Directions:

1. Mix simultaneously and serve.

2. Refrigerate if serve later. Unfinished portion should be disposed to avoid bacterial infection.

Fish and Quinoa Medley

Preparation time: 10 minutes

Cooking time: 22 minutes

Servings: 2

Ingredients:

- 1 cup white fish fillets (cooked and flaked)
- 1/2 cup cooked quinoa
- 1/4 cup carrots (grated)
- 1/4 cup spinach (severed)
- 1/2 tbsp fish oil

Directions:

1. Inside a big container, blend the flaked fish, cooked quinoa, grated carrots, severed spinach, and fish oil. Mix thoroughly.

2. Serve the medley to your dog at room temperature.

Lamb and Rice Stew

Preparation time: 14 minutes

Cooking time: 38 minutes

Servings: 3

Ingredients:

- 1/2 lb. lamb (cubed)
- 1 cup cooked white rice
- 1/4 cup carrots (finely severed)
- 1/4 cup green beans (severed)
- 1/8 cup peas
- 2 cups low-sodium vegetable broth

Directions:

1. Inside a big pot, brown the lamb across moderate flame.

2. Include carrots, green beans, peas, and vegetable broth to the pot. Stir well.

3. Boil, then diminish flame then simmer for thirty mins or till the lamb is soft.

4. Include the cooked rice to the pot. Stir till well combined.

5. Let the stew to cool prior to serving to your dog.

Pork and Sweet Potato Hash

Preparation time: 8 minutes

Cooking time: 23 minutes

Servings: 6

Ingredients:

- 1½ lbs ground pork
- 3 cups sweet potatoes (skinned and crushed)
- 1½ cup broccoli florets
- 1/3 cup blueberries
- 3 tbsps coconut oil

Directions:

1. Warm coconut oil in a huge griddle across moderate flame.

2. Include ground pork and cook till browned.

3. Include sweet potatoes and broccoli to the griddle. Cook till the vegetables are soft.

4. Stir in the blueberries and cook for a further two mins.

5. Let the hash to cool prior to serving to your dog.

Turkey and Sweet Potato Stew

Preparation time: 18 minutes

Cooking time: 40 minutes

Servings: 3

Ingredients:

- 1/2 lb. ground turkey
- 1 cup sweet potatoes (skinned and crushed)
- 1/2 cup green beans (trimmed and severed)
- 1/4 cup peas
- 2 cups low-sodium chicken broth
- 1 tbsp coconut oil

Directions:

1. Heat coconut oil in a huge pot across moderate flame.

2. Include ground turkey and cook till browned.

3. Include sweet potatoes, green beans, peas, and chicken broth to the pot. Stir well.

4. Boil, then diminish flame then simmer for thirty mins or 'til the sweet potatoes are soft.

5. Let the stew to cool prior to serving to your dog.

Beef and Barley Casserole

Preparation time: 14 minutes

Cooking time: 56 minutes

Servings: 4

Ingredients:

- 1/2 lb. lean ground beef
- 1/2 cup barley
- 1/4 cup carrots (finely severed)
- 1/4 cup peas
- 1/8 cup pumpkin puree
- 1½ cups low-sodium beef broth

Directions:

1. Warm up your oven to 350 deg. F.
2. Inside a huge griddle, brown the ground beef across moderate flame. Drain extra fat.
3. In a casserole dish, blend the cooked ground beef, barley, carrots, peas, pumpkin puree, and beef broth. Stir well.
4. Close the dish with foil then bake for one hr or 'til the barley is soft.
5. Let the casserole to cool prior to serving to your dog.

Chicken and Lentil Stew

Preparation time: 16 minutes

Cooking time: 44 minutes

Servings: 2

Ingredients:

- 1/3 lb. boneless, skinless chicken breasts (cubed)
- 1/3 cup lentils
- 1/4 cup carrots (finely severed)
- 1/4 cup green peas
- 1½ cups low-sodium chicken broth
- 1/2 tbsp olive oil

Directions:

1. Inside a huge pot, warm olive oil across moderate flame.
2. Include chicken cubes and cook till no longer pink.
3. Include lentils, carrots, green peas, and chicken broth to the pot. Stir well.
4. Boil, then diminish flame then simmer for thirty mins or till the lentils are cooked.

Turkey and Rice Medley

Preparation time: 17 minutes

Cooking time: 25 minutes

Servings: 8

Ingredients:

- 4 cups cooked ground turkey
- 2 cups cooked brown rice
- 1 cup carrots (grated)
- 1 cup peas
- 4 tbsps parsley (severed)

Directions:

1. Inside a big container, blend the ground turkey, cooked rice, grated carrots, peas, and severed parsley. Mix thoroughly.

2. Serve the medley to your dog at room temperature.

Duck and Potato Casserole

Preparation time: 20 minutes

Cooking time: 58 minutes

Servings: 3

Ingredients:

- 1 lb. duck meat (cubed)
- 1 cup potatoes (skinned and crushed)
- 1/2 cup carrots (finely severed)
- 1/4 cup green beans (severed)
- 1/8 cup blueberries
- 2 cups low-sodium chicken broth
- 1 tbsp olive oil

Directions:

1. Warm up your oven to 350 deg. F.

2. In your huge griddle, warm olive oil across moderate flame.

3. Include duck meat and brown on all sides.

4. In a casserole dish, blend the browned duck meat, potatoes, carrots, green beans, blueberries, and chicken broth. Stir well.

5. Close the dish with foil then bake for one hr or till the duck is cooked complete and the vegetables are soft.

6. Let the casserole to cool prior to serving to your dog.

Chicken and Quinoa Pilaf

Preparation time: 17 minutes

Cooking time: 28 minutes

Servings: 6

Ingredients:

- 3 cups cooked chicken (shredded)
- 1½ cups cooked quinoa
- 3/4 cup broccoli florets
- 3/4 cup carrots (grated)
- 3 tbsps coconut oil

Directions:

1. Inside a huge griddle, warm coconut oil across moderate flame.

2. Include broccoli florets and grated carrots. Cook for 5 minutes or till soft.

3. Include shredded chicken and cooked quinoa to the griddle. Stir well to blend.

4. Cook for an extra ten mins, mixing irregularly.

5. Let the pilaf to cool prior to serving to your dog.

Beef and Sweet Potato Stew

Preparation time: 18 minutes

Cooking time: 55 minutes

Servings: 4

Ingredients:

- 1 lb. beef stew meat (cubed)
- 1 cup sweet potatoes, skinned and crushed
- 1/2 cup carrots (severed)
- 1/4 cup peas
- 1/8 cup parsley (severed)
- 2 cups low-sodium beef broth
- 1 tbsp olive oil

Directions:

1. Inside a big pot, warm olive oil across moderate flame.

2. Include beef stew meat and brown on all sides.

3. Include sweet potatoes, carrots, peas, parsley, and beef broth to the pot. Stir well.

4. Boil, then diminish flame then simmer for one hr or till the beef is soft.

5. Let the stew to cool prior to serving to your dog.

Salmon and Rice Pilaf

Preparation time: 11 minutes

Cooking time: 26 minutes

Servings: 2

Ingredients:

- 1 cup cooked salmon (flaked)
- 1/2 cup cooked white rice
- 1/4 cup carrots (finely severed)
- 1/4 cup zucchini (crushed)
- 1 tbsp fish oil

Directions:

1. Inside a big container, blend the flaked salmon, cooked rice, severed carrots, crushed zucchini, and fish oil. Mix thoroughly.

2. Serve the pilaf to your dog at room temperature.

Lamb and Quinoa Stew

Preparation time: 16 minutes

Cooking time: 42 minutes

Servings: 6

Ingredients:

- 1 lb. lamb (cubed)
- 2 cups cooked quinoa
- 1/2 cup sweet potatoes (skinned and crushed)
- 1/2 cup zucchini (crushed)
- 4 cups low-sodium vegetable broth
- 2 tbsps coconut oil

Directions:

1. Inside a big pot, warm coconut oil across moderate flame.

2. Include lamb cubes and cook till browned.

3. Include cooked quinoa, sweet potatoes, zucchini, and vegetable broth to the pot. Stir well.

4. Boil, then diminish flame then simmer for thirty mins or till the lamb is soft.

5. Let the stew to cool prior to serving to your dog.

TREATS RECIPES

Chicken and Rice Balls

Preparation time: 16 minutes

Cooking time: 24 minutes

Servings: 25-30 balls

Ingredients:

- 2 cups cooked chicken (shredded)
- 2 cups cooked rice (white or brown)
- 1 cup grated carrots
- 1/2 cup chicken broth (low sodium)

Directions:

1. Warm up the oven to 350 deg. F then conceal a baking surface with parchment paper.
2. Inside your mixing container, blend the shredded chicken, cooked rice, and grated carrots.
3. Gradually include chicken broth to dampen the solution.
4. Roll the solution into small balls then put them on the organized baking surface.
5. Bake for twenty to twenty-five mins 'til the balls are cooked through.
6. Cool prior to serving or storing.

Blueberry Yogurt Drops

Preparation time: 6 minutes

Cooking time: 2 hours (chilling time)

Servings: variable

Ingredients:

- 3 cups plain Greek yogurt
- 1½ cups fresh blueberries

Directions:

1. Line a baking surface with parchment paper.
2. In your blender or mixing container, blend the plain Greek yogurt and fresh blueberries till uniform.
3. Pour the solution into a plastic sandwich bag or piping bag.
4. Cut a small hole in 1 corner of the bag to create a makeshift piping bag.
5. Squeeze small drops onto the arranged baking surface.
6. Take the baking surface in the freezer for around two hrs till the drops are frozen.
7. Eliminate from the freezer and transfer the drops to a sealed container.

Spinach and Cheese Bones

Preparation time: 16 minutes

Cooking time: 22 minutes

Servings: 20-25 treats

Ingredients:

- 2 cups whole wheat flour
- 1/2 cup cooked spinach (severed)
- 1/2 cup shredded cheddar cheese
- 1/4 cup unsweetened applesauce
- 1/4 cup water

Directions:

1. Warm up the oven to 350 deg. F then put a sheet of parchment paper on a baking tray.
2. Inside your mixing container, blend the whole wheat flour, cooked spinach, shredded cheddar cheese, applesauce, and water.
3. Mix thoroughly 'til all ingredients are thoroughly combined and form a dough.
4. Roll out the dough on a floured surface to about quarter inch denseness.
5. Cut out bone shapes using a cookie cutter then put them on the arranged baking surface.
6. Bake for twenty to twenty-five mins till the bones are firm and mildly browned.
7. Cool entirely prior to serving or storing.

Banana Coconut Bites

Preparation time: 17 minutes

Cooking time: 15 minutes

Servings: 40-45 treats

Ingredients:

- 4 ripe bananas (mashed)
- 1/2 cup coconut flour
- 1/2 cup rolled oats
- 1/2 cup shredded coconut (unsweetened)

Directions:

1. Warm up the oven to 350 deg. F then put a sheet of parchment paper on a baking tray.
2. Inside your mixing container, blend the mashed bananas, coconut flour, rolled oats, and shredded coconut.
3. Mix thoroughly 'til all ingredients are thoroughly combined.
4. Scoop out tablespoon-sized portions of the solution then shape them into small balls.
5. Transfer the balls on the arranged baking surface and level them mildly.
6. Bake for twelve to fifteen mins till the bites are firm and mildly golden.
7. Cool entirely prior to serving or storing.

Chicken Liver Jerky

Preparation time: 12 minutes

Cooking time: 4 hours

Servings: variable

Ingredients:

- 2 lbs chicken liver
- 1/2 cup low sodium chicken broth

Directions:

1. Warm up the oven to 200 deg. F then conceal a baking surface with parchment paper.
2. Rinse the chicken liver under cold water and pat dry.
3. Cut the liver into thin, even slices.
4. Put the liver slices in a shallow dish and pour the chicken broth over them.
5. Let the liver to marinate in the broth for ten mins.
6. Eliminate the liver slices from the broth and put them on the arranged baking surface.
7. Bake for four hrs till the liver is dried and crispy.
8. Let the jerky to cool entirely prior to serving or storing.

Peanut Butter Banana Bites

Preparation time: 10 minutes

Cooking time: -

Servings: 25-30 treats

Ingredients:

- 2 ripe bananas
- 1 cup natural peanut butter (no xylitol)
- 2 cups rolled oats

Directions:

1. Mash the banana in a container 'til uniform.
2. Include peanut butter and rolled oats, and mix well.
3. Roll the solution into small balls or shape them using a cookie cutter.
4. Take the treats on a baking surface lined with parchment paper.
5. Freeze for around two hrs till firm.
6. Keep it in a freezer-safe container that is sealed tightly.

Apple Cinnamon Biscuits

Preparation time: 14 minutes

Cooking time: 15 minutes

Servings: 10-12 treats

Ingredients:

- 1 cup whole wheat flour
- 1/4 cup unsweetened applesauce
- 1/8 cup unsweetened apple juice
- 1/2 tsp ground cinnamon (no more)
- 1/8 cup water (as needed)

Directions:

1. Warm up the oven to 350 deg. F then conceal a baking surface with parchment paper.
2. Inside your mixing container, blend the whole wheat flour and ground cinnamon.
3. Include the applesauce and apple juice to the dry ingredients and mix well.
4. Gradually include water as needed to establish a firm dough.
5. Roll out the dough to about quarter inch denseness on a floured surface.
6. Cut out biscuit shapes using a cookie cutter then transfer them on the arranged baking surface.
7. Bake for twenty mins or 'til the biscuits are golden brown.
8. Cool entirely prior to serving or storing.

Pumpkin and Cinnamon Cookies

Preparation time: 15 minutes

Cooking time: 15 minutes

Servings: 10-12 cookies

Ingredients:

- 1/2 cup canned pumpkin puree (unsweetened)
- 3/4 cup whole wheat flour
- 1/8 cup honey
- 1/2 tsp cinnamon (no more)

Directions:

1. Warm up the oven to 350 deg. F then put a sheet of parchment paper on a baking tray.
2. Inside your mixing container, blend the pumpkin puree, whole wheat flour, honey, and cinnamon.
3. Mix thoroughly 'til all ingredients are thoroughly combined and form a dough.
4. Roll out the dough on a floured surface to about quarter inch denseness.
5. Cut out cookie shapes using a cookie cutter then put them on the arranged baking surface.
6. Bake for twelve-fifteen mins 'til the cookies are firm and mildly browned.
7. Cool entirely prior to serving or storing.

Sweet Potato and Apple Biscuits

Preparation time: 14 minutes

Cooking time: 25 minutes

Servings: 40-45 treats

Ingredients:

- 2 cups cooked sweet potato (mashed)
- 1 cup unsweetened applesauce
- 4 cups whole wheat flour
- 1/2 cup water

Directions:

1. Warm up the oven to 350 deg. F then put a sheet of parchment paper on a baking tray.
2. Inside your mixing container, blend the mashed sweet potato, unsweetened applesauce, whole wheat flour, and water.
3. Mix thoroughly 'til all ingredients are thoroughly combined and form a dough.
4. Roll out the dough on a floured surface to about quarter inch denseness.
5. Cut out biscuit shapes using a cookie cutter then put them on the arranged baking surface.
6. Bake for twenty to twenty-five mins 'til the biscuits are firm and mildly browned.
7. Cool entirely prior to serving or storing.

Sweet Potato Chews

Preparation time: 6 minutes

Cooking time: 3 hours

Servings: variable

Ingredients:

- 3 medium-sized sweet potatoes

Directions:

1. Warm up the oven to 250 deg. F then conceal a baking surface with parchment paper.
2. Wash and dry the sweet potatoes.
3. Slice the sweet potatoes lengthwise into quarter-inch dense strips.
4. Place the strips on the baking surface, ensuring they do not overlap.
5. Bake for approximately 3 hours till the chews are dry and firm.
6. Let them to cool prior to serving.
7. Store in a sealed container.

Beef and Cheese Biscuits

Preparation time: 14 minutes

Cooking time: 25 minutes

Servings: 10-12 treats

Ingredients:

- 1/2 cup whole wheat flour
- 1/4 cup ground beef (cooked and drained)
- 1/4 cup shredded cheddar cheese
- 1/8 cup water
- 1/8 cup unsweetened applesauce

Directions:

1. Warm up the oven to 350 deg. F then put a sheet of parchment paper on a baking tray.
2. Inside your mixing container, blend the whole wheat flour, ground beef, shredded cheddar cheese, water, and applesauce.
3. Mix thoroughly 'til the ingredients are thoroughly combined and form a dough.
4. Roll out the dough on a floured surface to about quarter inch denseness.
5. Cut out biscuit shapes using a cookie cutter and transfer them on the arranged baking surface.
6. Bake for twenty to twenty-five mins 'til the biscuits are golden brown.
7. Cool entirely prior to serving or storing.

Salmon and Quinoa Balls

Preparation time: 16 minutes

Cooking time: 25 minutes

Servings: 25-30 balls

Ingredients:

- 2 cups canned salmon (boneless, skinless)
- 1 cup cooked quinoa
- 1/2 cup grated zucchini
- 1/2 cup grated carrots
- 2 eggs (whisked)

Directions:

1. Warm up the oven to 350 deg. F then conceal a baking surface with parchment paper.
2. Inside a mixing container, blend the canned salmon, cooked quinoa, grated zucchini, grated carrots, and whisked egg.
3. Mix thoroughly 'til all ingredients are thoroughly combined.
4. Roll the solution into small balls then put them on the arranged baking surface.
5. Bake for twenty to twenty-five mins 'til the balls are cooked through and mildly browned.
6. Let them to cool prior to serving.

Blueberry Pumpkin Muffins

Preparation time: 16 minutes

Cooking time: 20 minutes

Servings: 20-25 muffins

Ingredients:

- 3 cups whole wheat flour
- 3/4 cup canned pumpkin puree (unsweetened)
- 3/4 cup fresh blueberries
- 1/3 cup honey
- 1/3 cup unsweetened applesauce
- 3 eggs
- 1½ tsp baking powder
- 3/4 tsp cinnamon (no more)

Directions:

1. Warm up the oven to 350 deg. F then line a muffin tin with paper liners.
2. Inside your mixing container, blend the whole wheat flour, baking powder, and cinnamon.
3. Inside a different container, whisk together the pumpkin puree, honey, applesauce, and eggs.
4. Gradually put the wet components to the dry components, mixing till just combined.
5. Carefully wrap in the fresh blueberries.
6. Scoop the batter into the muffin tin, filling every cup around two-third.
7. Bake for 18-20 mins 'til the muffins are golden then a toothpick immersed into the middle comes out clean.
8. Cool entirely prior to serving.

Blueberry Coconut Ice Cream

Preparation time: 5 minutes

Freezing time: 6 hours

Servings: variable

Ingredients:

- 3 cups frozen blueberries
- 1½ cups coconut milk (full fat)
- 3 tbsps honey (optional)

Directions:

1. Inside your blender or mixing container, blend the frozen blueberries, coconut milk, and honey (if using) 'til uniform & creamy.
2. Transfer the solution into a freezer safe container.
3. Close then freeze for around six hrs or overnight 'til the ice cream is firm.
4. Let the ice cream to soften for a few minutes prior to serving.

Pumpkin and Oat Bites

Preparation time: 8 minutes

Cooking time: 12 minutes

Servings: 12-15 treats

Ingredients:

- 1/2 cup canned pumpkin puree (unsweetened)
- 3/4 cup rolled oats
- 1/8 cup coconut flour
- 1/8 cup unsweetened applesauce

Directions:

1. Warm up the oven to 350 deg. F then put a sheet of parchment paper on a baking tray.
2. Inside your mixing container, blend the pumpkin puree, rolled oats, coconut flour, and applesauce.
3. Mix thoroughly 'til all ingredients are thoroughly combined.
4. Scoop out tablespoon-sized portions of the solution then shape them into small balls.
5. Take the balls on the arranged baking surface and level them mildly.
6. Bake for ten-twelve mins till the bites are firm.
7. Cool entirely prior to serving or storing.

Carrot and Oat Biscuits

Preparation time: 12 minutes

Cooking time: 20 minutes

Servings: 40-45 treats

Ingredients:

- 2 cups grated carrots
- 2 cups rolled oats
- 1/2 cup unsweetened applesauce
- 1/2 cup water

Directions:

1. Warm up the oven to 350 deg. F then put a sheet of parchment paper on a baking tray.
2. Inside a mixing container, blend the grated carrots, rolled oats, applesauce, and water.
3. Mix thoroughly 'til all ingredients are thoroughly combined and form a dough.
4. Roll out the dough on a floured surface to about quarter inch denseness.
5. Cut out biscuit shapes using a cookie cutter then put them on the arranged baking surface.
6. Bake for eighteen-twenty mins 'til the biscuits are firm and mildly browned.
7. Cool entirely prior to serving or storing.

Turkey and Cranberry Meatballs

Preparation time: 20 minutes

Cooking time: 20 minutes

Servings: 12-15 meatballs

Ingredients:

- 2 lbs ground turkey
- 1/2 cup dried cranberries (unsweetened)
- 1/2 cup oat flour (you can make your own by blending rolled oats)
- 1/2 cup grated Parmesan cheese
- 1 egg (whisked)

Directions:

1. Warm up the oven to 375 deg. F then conceal a baking surface with parchment paper.
2. Inside your mixing container, blend the ground turkey, dried cranberries, oat flour, grated Parmesan cheese, and whisked egg.
3. Mix thoroughly 'til all ingredients are thoroughly combined.
4. Roll the solution into golf ball-sized meatballs then put them on the arranged baking surface.
5. Bake for eighteen-twenty mins till the meatballs are cooked through and mildly browned.
6. Let them to cool prior to serving.

Carrot and Zucchini Bites

Preparation time: 8 minutes

Cooking time: 25 minutes

Servings: 10-15 treats

Ingredients:

- 1/2 cup grated carrots
- 1/2 cup grated zucchini
- 1 cup whole wheat flour
- 1/8 cup unsweetened applesauce
- 1/8 cup water

Directions:

1. Warm up the oven to 350 deg. F then put a sheet of parchment paper on a baking tray.
2. Inside a mixing container, blend the grated carrots, grated zucchini, whole wheat flour, applesauce, and water.
3. Mix thoroughly 'til the ingredients are thoroughly combined and form a dough.
4. Roll out the dough on a floured surface to about quarter inch denseness.
5. Cut out bite-sized shapes using a cookie cutter then transfer them on the arranged baking surface.
6. Bake for twenty to twenty-five mins till the bites are firm and mildly browned.

Peanut Butter and Banana Popsicles

Preparation time: 10 minutes

Freezing time: 4 hours

Servings: variable

Ingredients:

- 4 ripe bananas (mashed)
- 1 cup natural peanut butter
- 2 cups plain Greek yogurt
- 1/2 cup water

Directions:

1. Inside your mixing container, blend the mashed bananas, peanut butter, Greek yogurt, and water.
2. Mix thoroughly 'til all ingredients are thoroughly combined.
3. Transfer the solution into popsicle molds or ice cube trays.
4. Place popsicle sticks into the molds or insert toothpicks into the ice cube trays.
5. Freeze for around four hrs till the popsicles are set.
6. Eliminate from the freezer and enjoy!

Raw Dog Treats

Preparation time: 18 minutes

Cooking time: -

Servings: 50-60 treats

Ingredients:

- 2 eggs
- 2 lbs ground sirloin
- 2 cups finely severed raw pumpkin seeds
- 4 tbsps molasses

Directions:

1. Using parchment paper, line a cookie sheet.
2. Crack the egg into a big container. Include in sirloin and molasses. Mix thoroughly.
3. On a distinct parchment paper, pour out severed raw pumpkin seeds.
4. Pinch off small amounts of the meat solution then shape them into balls, about 1 inch in size. Then, roll the meatballs in severed pumpkin seeds.
5. Arrange balls neatly on the cookie sheet and freeze them overnight.
6. Once frozen, retrieve balls from the freezer and remove them from the cookie sheet then store them in plastic bags with zip top. Store in the freezer for a maximum of 6 months.

Almond Banana Dog Treat

Preparation time: 6 minutes

Freezing time: 1 hour

Servings: 3

Ingredients:

- 2¼ cups Greek yogurt
- 3 tbsps almond butter
- 1½ bananas (cut into slices)

Directions:

1. Melt the almond butter.
2. Mash the banana perfectly.
3. Combine the banana with the almond butter.
4. Include the Greek yogurt.
5. Mix thoroughly. Include to silicon mold.
6. Freeze for one hr or longer. They are ready to serve.

Peanut Butter and Banana Frozen Yogurt

Preparation time: 5 minutes

Freezing time: 4 hours

Servings: variable

Ingredients:

- 4 ripe bananas (mashed)
- 1 cup plain Greek yogurt
- 4 tbsps natural peanut butter

Directions:

1. Inside your mixing container, blend the mashed bananas, Greek yogurt, and peanut butter.
2. Mix thoroughly 'til all components are thoroughly combined.
3. Transfer the solution into ice cube trays or silicone molds.
4. Place in the fridge and freeze for around four hrs till the yogurt is set.
5. Eliminate from the freezer and transfer the frozen yogurt cubes to a sealed container.
6. Store in the freezer.

Apple and Cheddar Biscuits

Preparation time: 12 minutes

Cooking time: 25 minutes

Servings: 40-45 treats

Ingredients:

- 2 cups grated apple (without seeds and core)
- 2 cups shredded cheddar cheese
- 3 cups whole wheat flour
- 1/2 cup unsweetened applesauce
- 1/2 cup water

Directions:

1. Warm up the oven to 350 deg. F then put a sheet of parchment paper on a baking tray.
2. Inside a mixing container, blend the grated apple, shredded cheddar cheese, whole wheat flour, applesauce, and water.
3. Mix thoroughly 'til all components are thoroughly combined and form a dough.
4. Roll out the dough on a floured surface to about quarter inch denseness.
5. Cut out biscuit shapes using a cookie cutter then put them on the arranged baking surface.
6. Bake for twenty-two to twenty-five mins till the biscuits are firm and mildly browned.
7. Cool entirely prior to serving or storing.

Carob and Peanut Butter Truffles

Preparation time: 14 minutes

Freezing time: 1 hour

Servings: variable

Ingredients:

- 2 cups peanut butter (unsalted and unsweetened)
- 1/2 cup carob powder
- 4 tbsps honey
- 1/2 cup oat flour

Directions:

1. Inside your mixing container, blend the peanut butter, carob powder, honey, and oat flour.
2. Mix thoroughly 'til all components are thoroughly combined and form a dough-like consistency.
3. Shape the dough into small truffles then put them on a baking surface lined with parchment paper.
4. Refrigerate the truffles for around one hr till firm.
5. Eliminate from the fridge and serve.

Spinach and Cheese Muffins

Preparation time: 13 minutes

Cooking time: 20 minutes

Servings: 20-25 muffins

Ingredients:

- 2 cups cooked spinach (severed)
- 2 cups shredded cheddar cheese
- 3 cups whole wheat flour
- 1 cup unsweetened applesauce
- 1/2 cup water

Directions:

1. Warm up the oven to 375 deg. F then line a muffin tin with paper liners.
2. Inside your mixing container, blend the cooked spinach, shredded cheddar cheese, whole wheat flour, applesauce, and water.
3. Mix thoroughly 'til all components are thoroughly mixed.
4. Scoop the batter into the muffin tin, filling every cup around two-third.
5. Bake for eighteen-twenty mins 'til the muffins are firm and mildly browned.
6. Let them to cool entirely prior to serving.

Chicken and Sweet Potato Patties

Preparation time: 16 minutes

Cooking time: 20 minutes

Servings: 35-45 patties

Ingredients:

- 3 cups cooked chicken (shredded)
- 3 cups cooked sweet potato (mashed)
- 3/4 cup oat flour
- 3/4 cup grated Parmesan cheese
- 3 eggs (whisked)

Directions:

1. Warm up the oven to 375 deg. F then put a sheet of parchment paper on a baking tray.
2. Inside a mixing container, blend the cooked chicken, mashed sweet potato, oat flour, grated Parmesan cheese, and whisked egg.
3. Mix thoroughly 'til all components are thoroughly combined.
4. Shape the solution into small patties then put them on the arranged baking surface.
5. Bake for eighteen-twenty mins till the patties are cooked through and mildly browned.
6. Let them to cool prior to serving.

Turkey and Vegetable Stir-Fry

Preparation time: 14 minutes

Cooking time: 15 minutes

Servings: 6

Ingredients:

- 3/4 lbs ground turkey
- 3/4 cup severed green beans
- 3/4 cup crushed zucchini
- 1/3 cup grated carrots
- 1/3 cup peas
- 1½ tbsps olive oil
- 1½ tsp low-sodium soy sauce

Directions:

1. Warm the olive oil in your griddle across moderate flame.
2. Include the ground turkey to the griddle then cook till browned.
3. Include the green beans, zucchini, grated carrots, and peas to the griddle.
4. Stir-fry the solution for around eight-ten mins till the vegetables are soft.
5. Include the soy sauce and mix well.
6. Let the stir-fry to cool prior to serving.

Turkey and Pumpkin Meatballs

Preparation time: 8 minutes

Cooking time: 20 minutes

Servings: 10-15 meatballs

Ingredients:

- 1/2 lb. ground turkey
- 1/4 cup canned pumpkin puree (unsweetened)
- 1/8 cup grated carrots
- 1/8 cup severed parsley

Directions:

1. Warm up the oven to 375 deg. F then conceal a baking surface with parchment paper.
2. Inside your mixing container, blend the ground turkey, pumpkin puree, grated carrots, and severed parsley.
3. Mix thoroughly 'til all components are thoroughly combined.
4. Roll the solution into small meatballs then put them on the arranged baking surface.
5. Bake for eighteen-twenty mins till the meatballs are cooked through and mildly browned.
6. Let them to cool prior to serving.

Blueberry and Coconut Bites

Preparation time: 8 minutes

Cooking time: 15 minutes

Servings: 40-50 bites

Ingredients:

- 2 cups blueberries
- 1 cup coconut flour
- 1/2 cup coconut oil (melted)
- 4 eggs

Directions:

1. Warm up the oven to 350 deg. F then put a sheet of parchment paper on a baking tray.
2. Inside your mixing container, mash the blueberries using a fork or blender till you have a uniform puree.
3. Include the coconut flour, melted coconut oil, and eggs to the container.
4. Mix thoroughly 'til all components are thoroughly combined and form a dough-like consistency.
5. Roll the dough into small bite-sized balls then put them on the arranged baking surface.
6. Bake for twelve-fifteen mins till the bites are firm and mildly golden.
7. Let them to cool prior to serving.

Baked Oat Veggie Treats

Preparation time: 7 minutes

Cooking time: 15 minutes

Servings: 3

Ingredients:

- 1 egg
- 1/2 cup oats
- 1/2 carrot (shredded)
- 6 basil leaves (severed)
- 1/4 tsp cinnamon (no more)
- 1/6 tsp cumin

Directions:

1. Grease a muffin tray using oil.
2. In a mixing container, beat the eggs.
3. Include the cinnamon and cumin.
4. Include the oats, carrots, and basil. Mix thoroughly.
5. Include the solution to the muffin tray. Spread the top evenly.
6. Bake for fifteen mins. Serve.

Beef and Rice Stuffed Bell Peppers

Preparation time: 22 minutes

Cooking time: 35 minutes

Servings: four 8 stuffed peppers

Ingredients:

- 8 bell peppers (any color), halved and seeds removed
- 1 pound ground beef
- 1 cup cooked rice
- 1/2 cup grated carrots
- 1/2 cup severed parsley

Directions:

1. Warm up the oven to 375 deg. F.
2. In a griddle, cook the ground beef over medium warm till browned. Drain any extra fat.
3. In a mixing container, blend the cooked ground beef, cooked rice, grated carrots, and severed parsley.
4. Mix thoroughly 'til all components are thoroughly combined.
5. Fill each bell pepper half with the beef and rice solution.
6. Place the stuffed peppers on a baking dish and cover with foil.
7. Bake for twenty-five mins, then remove the foil and bake for a further ten mins.
8. Let them to cool prior to serving.

Salmon Balls

Preparation time: 18 minutes

Cooking time: 15 minutes

Servings: 30-35 balls

Ingredients:

- 3 cups cooked brown rice
- 4½ cups cooked salmon (severed)
- 3 tbsps olive oil
- 3 eggs

Directions:

1. Warm up your oven to 350 deg. F. Cover a baking surface with parchment paper.
2. Mixed all the components in a mixing container and mix thoroughly. Form 30-35 balls out of the solution. Arrange neatly on the cookie sheet.
3. Place in the oven then bake for ten-fifteen mins. Make sure to let the treats cool down entirely prior to you serve them or put them in the fridge.
4. Keep in the refrigerator for 3-4 days or store in a sealed container in the freezer for up to 6 months.

Homemade Applesauce Dog Treats

Preparation time: 12 minutes

Cooking time: 25 minutes

Servings: 2

Ingredients:

- 1/2 cup unsweetened applesauce
- 1½ cups wheat flour
- 1/2 egg
- 1/4 cup water
- 1/2 tsp. cinnamon (no more)

Directions:

1. Include the entire components into a container then mix thoroughly.
2. Pour into molds. Place in the oven. Bake for twenty to twenty-five mins at 350 deg. F.
3. Let to cool entirely and serve.

Chicken and Broccoli Casserole

Preparation time: 16 minutes

Cooking time: 25 minutes

Servings: 8

Ingredients:

- 2 cups cooked chicken (shredded)
- 2 cups cooked broccoli (severed)
- 1 cup low-sodium chicken broth
- 1 cup plain Greek yogurt
- 1/2 cup grated Parmesan cheese
- 1/2 cup whole wheat breadcrumbs

Directions:

1. Warm up the oven to 375 deg. F and oil a baking dish.
2. In a mixing container, blend the cooked chicken, cooked broccoli, chicken broth, Greek yogurt, and grated Parmesan cheese.
3. Mix thoroughly 'til all components are thoroughly mixed.
4. Pour the solution to the greased baking dish then spread it evenly.
5. Pour the breadcrumbs on top of the casserole.
6. Bake for twenty to twenty-five mins 'til the casserole is heated through and the breadcrumbs are golden
7. Let it to cool prior to serving.

Turkey and Quinoa Stuffed Bell Peppers

Preparation time: 22 minutes

Cooking time: 35 minutes

Servings: four 8 stuffed peppers

Ingredients:

- 8 bell peppers (any color), halved and seeds removed
- 1 lb. ground turkey
- 1 cup cooked quinoa
- 1/2 cup severed bell pepper
- 1/2 cup tomato sauce
- 1/2 tsp dried oregano
- 2/3 tsp dried basil

Directions:

1. Warm up the oven to 375 deg. F.
2. In a griddle, cook the ground turkey across moderate flame till browned. Drain any extra fat.
3. In the same griddle, put the bell pepper. Sauté for a few minutes till softened.
4. Include the cooked quinoa, tomato sauce, dried oregano, and dried basil to the griddle. Stir well to blend.
5. Fill each bell pepper half with the turkey and quinoa solution.
6. Place the stuffed peppers on a baking dish and cover with foil.
7. Bake for twenty-five mins and then remove the foil then bake for further ten mins.
8. Let them to cool prior to serving.

Banana and Yogurt Frozen Drops

Preparation time: 12 minutes

Freezing time: 3 hours

Servings: variable

Ingredients:

- 5 ripe bananas (mashed)
- 2½ cups plain Greek yogurt

Directions:

1. Inside your mixing container, blend the mashed bananas and Greek yogurt.
2. Mix thoroughly 'til all components are thoroughly combined.
3. Spoon small drops of the solution onto a parchment-lined baking surface.
4. Place the baking surface in the freezer then freeze for around 3 hours till the drops are firm.
5. Eliminate from the freezer and enjoy!

RECIPES FOR DOGS WITH SPECIFIC DIETARY NEEDS

Salmon and Quinoa Medley (Skin and Coat Health)

Preparation time: 12 minutes

Cooking time: 23 minutes

Servings: 4

Ingredients:

- 2 cups cooked salmon (flaked)
- 1 cup cooked quinoa
- 1/2 cup cooked green beans (severed)
- 1/4 cup cooked carrots (grated)
- 1 tbsp flaxseed oil

Directions:

1. Inside a big container, blend the cooked salmon, quinoa, green beans, and carrots.

2. Drizzle flaxseed oil over the solution and toss till well-coated.

3. Let the solution to cool prior to serving.

Beef and Pumpkin Stew (Weight Management)

Preparation time: 13 minutes

Cooking time: 56 minutes

Servings: 6

Ingredients:

- 1½ lbs lean ground beef
- 1½ cups canned pumpkin puree
- 3/4 cup cooked barley
- 1/3 cup cooked spinach (severed)
- 1/3 cup low-sodium beef broth

Directions:

1. Inside a big pot, brown the ground beef across moderate flame till cooked through.

2. Drain extra fat and include the pumpkin puree, barley, spinach, and beef broth.

3. Stir well and simmer for forty mins, mixing occasionally.

4. Cool prior to serving to your dog.

Chicken and Oatmeal Casserole (Joint Health)

Preparation time: 15 minutes

Cooking time: 45 minutes

Servings: 8

Ingredients:

- 4 cups cooked chicken (shredded)
- 2 cups cooked oatmeal
- 1 cup cooked carrots (finely severed)
- 1/2 cup cooked green peas
- 1/2 cup low-sodium chicken broth
- 2 tbsps fish oil

Directions:

1. Warm up the oven to 375 deg. F.

2. Inside a big container, blend the cooked chicken, oatmeal, carrots, green peas, chicken broth, and fish oil.

3. Mix till well combined.

4. Pour the solution into a baking dish then spread evenly.

5. Bake for thirty to thirty-five mins or 'til mildly browned on top.

6. Let the casserole to cool prior to serving.

Lamb and Sweet Potato Stew (Allergies)

Preparation time: 17 minutes

Cooking time: 54 minutes

Servings: 6

Ingredients:

- 1½ lbs ground lamb
- 1½ cups cooked sweet potatoes (mashed)
- 3/4 cup cooked green beans (severed)
- 1/3 cup cooked peas
- 1/3 cup low-sodium lamb broth

Directions:

1. Inside a big pot, brown the ground lamb across moderate flame till cooked through.

2. Drain extra fat and include the mashed sweet potatoes, green beans, peas, and lamb broth.

3. Stir well and simmer for forty mins, mixing occasionally.

4. Let the stew to cool prior to serving.

Duck and Pumpkin Stew (Sensitive Stomach)

Preparation time: 14 minutes

Cooking time: 52 minutes

Servings: 4

Ingredients:

- 1 lb. ground duck
- 1 cup cooked pumpkin puree
- 1/2 cup cooked barley
- 1/4 cup cooked green beans (severed)
- 1/4 cup low-sodium duck broth

Directions:

5. Inside a big pot, brown the ground duck across moderate flame till cooked through.

6. Drain extra fat and include the pumpkin puree, cooked barley, green beans, and duck broth.

7. Stir well and simmer for forty mins, mixing occasionally.

8. Let the stew to cool prior to serving.

Bison and Sweet Potato Stew (Weight Management)

Preparation time: 18 minutes

Cooking time: 56 minutes

Servings: 8

Ingredients:

- 2 lbs ground bison
- 2 cups cooked sweet potatoes (mashed)
- 1 cup cooked quinoa
- 1/2 cup cooked green beans (severed)
- 1/2 cup low-sodium beef broth

Directions:

1. Inside a big pot, brown the ground bison across moderate flame till cooked through.

2. Drain extra fat and include the mashed sweet potatoes, cooked quinoa, green beans, and beef broth.

3. Stir well and simmer for forty mins, mixing occasionally.

4. Cool prior to serving to your dog.

Turkey and Quinoa Patties (Digestive Health)

Preparation time: 22 minutes

Cooking time: 30 minutes

Servings: 30-35 patties

Ingredients:

- 3 lbs ground turkey
- 3 cups cooked quinoa
- 1½ cups cooked pumpkin (mashed)
- 3/4 cup cooked carrots (finely severed)
- 3/4 cup fresh parsley (severed)

Directions:

1. Warm up the oven to 375 deg. F then put a sheet of parchment paper on a baking tray.

2. In your huge container, blend the ground turkey, cooked quinoa, pumpkin, carrots, and parsley.

3. Mix the components till well combined.

4. Shape the solution into patties then put them on the arranged baking surface.

5. Bake for 25-thirty mins or 'til cooked through.

6. Let the patties to cool entirely prior to serving.

Whitefish and Brown Rice Stir-Fry (Digestive Health)

Preparation time: 10 minutes

Cooking time: 24 minutes

Servings: 4-6

Ingredients:

- 3 cups cooked whitefish (flaked)
- 1½ cups cooked brown rice
- 3/4 cup cooked broccoli (severed)
- 1/3 cup cooked carrots (grated)
- 1½ tbsps coconut oil

Directions:

1. Inside a big griddle, warm the coconut oil across moderate flame.

2. Include the cooked whitefish, brown rice, broccoli, and carrots to the griddle.

3. Stir-fry for five to seven mins till heated through and well combined.

4. Let the stir-fry to cool prior to serving.

Chicken and Rice Delight (Sensitive Stomach)

Preparation time: 8 minutes

Cooking time: 36 minutes

Servings: 3

Ingredients:

- 2 cups cooked chicken (shredded)
- 1 cup cooked brown rice
- 1 cup cooked sweet potatoes (mashed)
- 1/2 cup cooked carrots (finely severed)
- 1/4 cup cooked peas
- 1 tbsp olive oil

Directions:

1. Inside a big container, blend all the components.

2. Mix thoroughly till thoroughly combined.

3. Serve the desired portion to your dog after it has cooled.

Tofu and Vegetable Stir-Fry (Vegetarian/Vegan)

Preparation time: 14 minutes

Cooking time: 17 minutes

Servings: 8

Ingredients:

- 2 cups tofu (cubed)
- 2 cups cooked quinoa
- 1 cup cooked broccoli (severed)
- 1/2 cup cooked carrots (grated)
- 1/2 cup cooked peas
- 4 tbsps soy sauce
- 2 tbsps sesame oil

Directions:

1. Inside a big griddle, warm the sesame oil across moderate flame.

2. Include the tofu, quinoa, broccoli, carrots, and peas to the griddle.

3. Stir-fry for five to seven mins till heated through.

4. Drizzle soy sauce over the stir-fry and toss till well-coated.

5. Let the stir-fry to cool prior to serving.

CONCLUSION

In today's fast-paced world, many pet owners are seeking alternatives to commercial dog food and exploring homemade options for their furry friends. The idea of preparing healthy meals for your dog can be an exciting and rewarding endeavor. Not only does it allow you to have complete control over the components, but it also provides an opportunity to nourish your dog with wholesome, nutritious meals tailored to their specific needs. The homemade healthy dog food cookbook serves as a valuable resource to guide you through this culinary journey.

Throughout this cookbook, we have explored a wide array of recipes, highlighting the importance of balanced nutrition for dogs. We have emphasized the significance of incorporating high-quality protein sources, nutrient-rich vegetables, and healthy fats into their diet. By following these recipes, you can ensure that your dog receives a well-rounded and wholesome diet, free from artificial additives and preservatives.

The benefits of homemade dog food extend far beyond the nutritional aspect. By preparing meals for your dog, you establish a deeper connection and bond. Sharing a home-cooked meal not only provides nourishment but also creates a sense of love and care that can be felt by your beloved canine companion. Additionally, preparing homemade meals can be a creative outlet, allowing you to experiment with different flavors and components to cater to your dog's preferences.

While the idea of homemade dog food may seem daunting at first, it's essential to approach it with confidence and an open mind. The recipes provided in this cookbook are designed to be simple and accessible, even for those with limited culinary experience. Remember, the goal is not to achieve culinary perfection but rather to provide your dog with a nutritious and balanced diet.

As you embark on this journey, there are a few key points to keep in mind:

1. Consult with Your Veterinarian: Before making any changes to your dog's diet, it is crucial to consult with your veterinarian. They can offer valuable insights based on your dog's specific needs, such as allergies, dietary restrictions, or health conditions.

2. Balance and Variety: Just like humans, dogs benefit from a balanced and varied diet. Rotate the recipes in the cookbook and incorporate a range of proteins, vegetables, and healthy grains to ensure your dog receives a broad spectrum of nutrients.

3. Portion Control: Pay attention to portion sizes and adjust them according to your dog's age, weight, and activity level. Overfeeding can lead to weight gain and associated health issues, while underfeeding can result in nutrient deficiencies.

4. Gradual Transition: If you are transitioning your dog from commercial food to homemade meals, do it gradually over a period of 7-10 days to allow their digestive system to adjust.

5. Quality Ingredients: Use fresh, high-quality components whenever possible. Opt for organic products, and avoid components that may be harmful or toxic to dogs, such as onions, garlic, chocolate, and certain spices.

Remember, homemade dog food should not replace regular veterinary check-ups. Your veterinarian plays a vital role in monitoring your dog's overall health and can provide guidance and support throughout your homemade dog food journey.

So, why not take a leap of faith and explore the world of homemade healthy dog food? Not only will you be providing your furry friend with a nutritious and wholesome diet, but you will also experience the joy of nourishing them with your own hands. The homemade healthy dog food cookbook is here to inspire and guide you every step of the way. Embrace the adventure, and watch your dog thrive on a diet filled with love and nutritious goodness.

CONVERSION CHART

Volume Equivalents (Liquid)

US Standard	US Standard (ounces)	Metric (approximate)
2 tablespoons	1 fl. oz.	30 mL
¼ cup	2 fl. oz.	60 mL
½ cup	4 fl. oz.	120 mL
1 cup	8 fl. oz.	240 mL
1½ cups	12 fl. oz.	355 mL
2 cups or 1 pint	16 fl. oz.	475 mL
4 cups or 1 quart	32 fl. oz.	1 L

Volume Equivalents (Dry)

US Standard	Metric (approximate)
⅛ teaspoon	0.5 mL
¼ teaspoon	1 mL
½ teaspoon	2 mL
¾ teaspoon	4 mL
1 teaspoon	5 mL
1 tablespoon	15 mL
¼ cup	59 mL
⅓ cup	79 mL
½ cup	118 mL
⅔ cup	156 mL
¾ cup	177 mL
1 cup	235 mL
2 cups or 1 pint	475 mL
3 cups	700 mL

Oven Temperatures

Fahrenheit (F)	Celsius (C) (approximate)
250°F	120°C
300°F	150°C
325°F	165°C
350°F	180°C
375°F	190°C
400°F	200°C
425°F	220°C
450°F	230°C

Weight Equivalents

US Standard	Metric (approximate)
1 tablespoon	15 g
½ ounce	15 g
1 ounce	30 g
2 ounces	60 g
4 ounces	115 g
8 ounces	225 g
12 ounces	340 g
16 ounces or 1 pound	455 g

Printed in Great Britain
by Amazon

28934381R00057